HISTORICAL CATASTROPHES: VOLCANOES

AN ADDISONIAN PRESS BOOK

by Billye and Walter R. Brown

HISTORICAL CATASTROPHES:

VOLCANOES

A Addison-Wesley

The Addison-Wesley Publishing Company, Inc.
Reading, Massachusetts 01867

Library of Congress catalog card number 79-118992
Printed in the United States of America
First printing
SBN: 201-00741-X

CONTENTS

FOREWORD

WHY ALL THE FUSS about volcanoes? We read every newspaper story about new eruptions of volcanoes; we sit hypnotized in front of the television screen when there is a program about them. Almost every primitive group of people has legends about volcanoes. Novels have been written about them, and some movies include volcanoes as featured "actors."

Only a part of this interest comes from the destruction caused by volcanoes. During the recorded history of man, probably not more than 250,000 people have been killed by volcanoes—many fewer than the total killed by either earthquakes or floods.

And we are certainly not fascinated by volcanoes because of the number of people killed by a single eruption. The deadliest volcano was probably Tomboro, an island off the coast of Java that exploded in 1815. Perhaps as many as 80,000 people died as the result of this single eruption. But single earthquakes have killed perhaps ten times this many people, and floods have done even more damage.

It could be the dramatic nature of a volcano that excites us. When a volcano erupts, its force may be equal to the explosion of several hydrogen bombs. It may throw rocks weighing several tons for many miles. And then, part of the attraction could be because volcanoes may suddenly change the face of the earth with results that can be seen for centuries.

Perhaps another reason we read about volcanoes is our awe of things we don't understand. We hope this book will add to your understanding, as well as your excitement, about volcanoes. As you read about individually famous volcanic eruptions, you will see there are many different types. Some explode violently, lifting tons of earth into the sky. Others release clouds of poisonous gases that kill every living thing they touch. Others flow quietly, burying whole cities and their people.

But not all volcanoes destroy; some bring new, fertile soil to the mountainside and plains below. Whole towns are heated by volcanic heat; in several places electricity is produced with generators turned by volcanic steam. Volcanoes bring minerals to the surface that ordinarily would be too deep for men to reach.

The study of volcanoes *is* fascinating, not only for the young student, but also for the professional scientist. As you read about these volcanoes you will learn about many of the people who have studied them. There are scientists who want to know what causes a volcanic eruption. There are people who study volcanoes so they can predict when and where a future eruption may take place. There are scientists who study ruins of cities that have been covered with ash and lava. These ruins often show exactly how people lived hundreds and thousands of years ago.

Studying volcanoes can be an adventure—an adventure into the past, the present, and the future.

Billye Walker Brown
Walter R. Brown

Charlottesville, Virginia

CHAPTER ONE

THE EXPLOSION HEARD AROUND THE WORLD

MAY 20, 1883, SEEMED LIKE an ordinary day, full of bright tropic sunlight. The water of the Sunda Strait was alive with fish. Three fishermen in a tiny boat made their way slowly through the strait, a narrow neck of water that connects the Java Sea with the Indian Ocean.

The fishermen paddled their boat in a large circle, dropping their long net over the side. When the small, wooden floats were all strung out into a circle behind them, they slowly began pulling at the ropes that held both ends of the net. All three of the men had to lift the water-soaked and fish-filled net into the boat.

One of the fishermen paused in his work with the nets, straightening his tired back muscles. As he did, he glanced toward the nearby, deserted island called Krakatoa. At the top of the smallest of the island's three peaks hung a white cloud. Upon looking closer, the fisherman thought the cloud seemed to boil out of the top of the mountain.

He called to his friends, his voice tinged with curiosity and awe. The fishermen forgot the fish below and stared, fascinated by the scene. They had felt uneasy for several days because of the earthquakes that had been shaking their island. As they watched, the cloud of steam became steadily darker and more threatening, rising higher into the calm air. Their uneasiness turned to fear. Their hearts pounded and their knees felt weak. They were frozen with fright.

Suddenly, with a flash of light and a billow of smoke, the peak destroyed itself in a tremendous explosion. The fishermen were completely deafened and they cowered in the bottom of their boat, trying to protect themselves from the huge rocks that fell hissing into the water all around them.

The world did not need to wait for the fishermen to return to their village to learn of the activity on Krakatoa. The first explosion was heard over 100 miles away in the cities now called Djakarta and Bogor. The column of black dust that rose seven miles above the island was seen from miles away in all directions.

All over the world, *volcanologists* (scientists who study volcanoes) were excited at the news of the explosion, for until recently they had thought the island was an extinct (dead) volcano. At least, it *had* been extinct, lying quietly for many years. Its last period of activity had been in

1680, when a quiet flow of melted lava had destro
of the plants on the island. Between 1680 and 1883,
however, the volcano had been so quiet that new plants
had found root in the dirt that formed as the lava broke
apart. Gradually, the three peaks of the island were
again covered by a dense, tropical forest.

Since this area of the world had often been racked by
the most violent of volcanoes, the 1883 explosion did
not really surprise the volcanologists. They knew that
far beneath Krakatoa the temperatures were thousands
of degrees higher than on the surface. Rock was melting
there and as it did so it expanded, taking up more and
more space. The pressure on the crust under the island
was becoming greater and greater. If the pressure
from the expanding rock became great enough, the
crust would crack at its weakest point.

Sometime in the dim past, before men began writing
their history, a huge volcano that had stood in this
same spot was completely destroyed by what must have
been a tremendous explosion. Only a rim far below the
surface of the water was left, along with two small peaks
that formed tiny islands barely 400 feet high. Later,
huge flows of lava were released beneath the water.
Slowly a third mountain peak built up until it extended
for almost half a mile above the level of the sea. Further
quiet flows of lava joined the three peaks into a single
island which became known as Krakatoa.

In spite of the fact that the surface of the volcano had
been quiet for six generations, volcanologists were ex-
pecting new activity in the area of Krakatoa. For several
days before the May 20th explosion, the large islands of
both Java and Sumatra had been shaken by earth-

quakes. The scientists knew that these earthquakes were a sign that pressure was again building up somewhere below the islands.

Once the explosions on Krakatoa began, it seemed as if they would continue forever. About every ten minutes the smallest cone on the island gave a mighty roar, throwing dust and rocks into the air. The crews of passing ships complained that the brass on their ships became black from sulfur fumes that seemed to fill the air. People living over three hundred miles away constantly swept dust away from their houses.

By May 27, a week after the first explosion, the strength of the blasts became weaker, and a boatload of people visited the island. They found fumes coming from two large cracks in the ground. One of these *fissures* was about 30 feet across and steadily poured forth a swirling cloud of steam and dust. The visitors also noticed that all the plants were dead. The surface of the island was covered with a thick layer of fine dust.

Since the island of Krakatoa was uninhabited, it appeared that no damage had been done by the eruptions. The visitors finished their inspection, returned to their homes, and talked excitedly about what they had seen. But they did not realize they were to be the last people to visit the island—for it would soon disappear from the face of the earth!

During the summer, the little island was shaken by more small explosions, burying itself deeper and deeper in the choking ash that poured from cracks in its sides. The pressure under the island continued to increase. If the mountain had split more deeply into the mass of lava below, the lava might have flowed quietly out through the fissures. But in the two hundred years since the last eruption of this volcano, the old lava in its neck had cooled into solid rock—rock too hard to crack under the pressure from below. So the pressure became greater and greater.

Suddenly, in late August, Krakatoa was actually torn to pieces! The rocks gave way under the tremendous pressure, resulting in what may have been the world's loudest explosion. It has been estimated that five cubic miles of rock were pulverized and simply disappeared! Can you imagine a pile of rock and dirt, measuring one mile on each side and five miles high—almost as tall as the world's tallest mountain—being blown apart?

The first eye-witness report of this explosion came from a ship that was sailing about 75 miles from the island. Early in the afternoon of August 26, the sailor on forward watch reported to his commander a tremendous noise and a column of black "smoke." The captain later reported that the column of dust may have risen 15 or 20 miles into the sky.

Shortly after this, the people living in northern Java, over 100 miles away, began to hear the explosions. "What is that noise?" children asked their parents. "It is the volcano on Krakatoa," they were told. "Do not worry. It is a long way away. And it will stop soon."

But the explosions did not stop. Instead, they became louder and louder. The children became more and more afraid. They went to bed at nightfall, as they usually did, but the noise was so loud they could not sleep. Many of the smaller children began to cry as the sound of the explosions became even louder. By midnight they could not hear each other speak over the steady roar of the volcano. All night the people lay awake, feeling their houses shake and watching their windows rattle.

The ships at sea that night sailed through inky blackness that was cut only by lightning flashes, branching like the limbs of trees. These strange bolts of lightning are often seen near an erupting volcano. Scientists who study weather investigate this kind of lightning, hoping that it will help them to explain the lightning that comes with a storm.

One of these ships was manned by European officers and a crew of South Pacific islanders. It spent the night in the Bay of Lampong, about 50 miles from the rumbling volcano. As the ship slowly made its way through the gloom, a shower of ash mixed with rain fell upon it. Something in the rain of mud glowed in the dark, and soon the masts and decks of the ship appeared to be covered with millions of fireflies. One of the native crew members shouted that the light was the work of evil spirits. Someone else said that if the evil light found its way below decks it would eat through the bottom of the ship. With this, the terrified natives abandoned their posts and attempted to put the lights out by smothering them with their hands or throwing the mud overboard. Without a crew to stoke the boilers, the officers were helpless. Consequently, they had to spend the murky night watching the excited and anxious natives scramble across the slippery decks.

The steady roar and belching of fumes and rock from the volcano continued throughout the night, but the pressure from the depths below did not decrease. The mountain-island seemed to fight against it, opening new fissures and throwing its insides into the air. Then, as the sun rose out of the Java Sea on the morning of August 27, the mountain was racked by an explosion that was even louder than the steady roar that was now being heard over 200 miles away. An hour later, a second huge explosion shook the entire area, and then a calm settled. For three and a half hours, the people on the islands and the ships nearby waited anxiously, hoping it was over.

Then, a few minutes after 10 o'clock that morning, the earth tore apart with a force nearly as great as the largest earthquake. Much of the island was blown upward into the air. What was left sank below the surface of the water, so that parts of the island once 1000 feet above, now lay at least 1000 feet below sea level.

In any explosion there is noise, caused by the squeezing and sudden release of the air. The sound waves caused by the death of Krakatoa were possibly the loudest ever heard on earth. They traveled out in all directions at nearly 750 miles per hour. These waves of air broke windows and cracked cement walls for 200 miles in all directions. In Burma, almost 1500 miles away, a police boat was sent out to sea to investigate what the captain thought was the distant firing of guns, perhaps the signal of a ship calling for help. In western Australia, some 1700 miles to the southeast, the people sat and listened to what they thought was the sound of artillery firing for over five hours. The "guns of Krakatoa" were also heard on Rodriguez island, which lies off the coast of Africa, almost 3000 miles west of Krakatoa!

Long after the waves of air had lost enough strength to be heard by people, they continued to flow around the earth. *Barometers*, instruments that are used by weather men to measure slight changes in air pressure, showed that the waves of air reached central Europe about ten hours after the explosion. Less than a day and a half later, the waves again disturbed the barometers of Europe, showing that the shock of Krakatoa's explosion had traveled completely around the earth. Altogether, over the next nine days, the barometers showed the wave passing around the earth a total of four times!

What happened to the rock and dirt that had once been the island of Krakatoa? Some of it sank into the ocean. Probably more than four cubic miles of it were thrown into the air. Most of this material, of course, fell back into the turbulent sea. But some of it, in the form of dust and ash, was blown upward into the sky where it was caught in wind currents. For miles around, the sun was completely blotted out. Some reports say that the column of dust rose upward for 50 miles— well into the stratosphere.

Perhaps the dust plume didn't reach this tremendous height. We can't be certain, since there were no methods available then to actually measure it. But it did apparently reach the "jet stream" that we now know exists in some places in the stratosphere. The ash and dust were carried from the top of the cloud toward the northwest, spreading the darkness with it. Quickly the cloud scurried up and over Sumatra. Terrified villagers cowered in their homes as the ash rained down on them, hour after hour. For all of that day and part of the next, the sun wasn't visible.

On and on the lighter dust particles blew, settling everywhere and adding brilliant color to the sky at sunset. By September 2, some of it drifted down on the west coast of South America. On September 9, less than two weeks after the explosion that had started it, the first particles of dust and ash completely circled the earth and drifted down on the empty sea where Krakatoa had once stood.

Eventually bits of the island settled in every point in the world. But this final settling took years, and 24 months after the explosion, the citizens of every country could still see the effects of the dust in the air. Beautiful sunsets and sunrises were everywhere. Rainbows were seen long after sunset, as the light of the sun struck the tiny dust particles that had once been an island and were now floating many miles above the earth. At times, the sun appeared to be green or blue, and the moon often had a green halo.

As often happens during a volcanic eruption, Krakatoa produced a large amount of *pumice*, or "floating rock." Pumice is lava that has trapped some of the gas that bubbled up through it as it cooled and became solid. As a solid rock, it often looks like a piece of black sponge, full of holes and bubbles of gas. Since this rock is largely made of air-pockets, it is lighter than water and will actually float. For about 18 months after the explosion at Krakatoa, ships sailing through the Sunda Strait were forced to go slowly because the sea was covered with these floating rocks.

The sound waves that broke windows, the dust that caused beautiful sunsets, and the floating rocks that disturbed the movement of ships were not the only effects of the destruction of Krakatoa. Since no one

lived on the island, no human life was lost. But the force
of the explosion caused other waves, similar to the
sound waves. These waves, however, were in the water.

You have probably dropped a rock into a pond of
still water and seen the circle of waves that rush away
from it. In the same way, the explosions and collapse of
Krakatoa caused sea waves scientists call *tsunamis*.

Some of these waves were over 50 feet high in the
open ocean, and rushed out, away from the island, at
tremendous speeds—perhaps as fast as 350 miles per
hour. They moved across the open ocean until they
crashed upon a beach somewhere. All through Indonesia, tiny beachside villages were suddenly and unexpectedly swept away by these tsunamis. A 125-foot-high
wall of water swept the coast of Java, destroying 300
villages. In Sumatra, the situation was just as bad. One
village was covered by 80 feet of water, and everyone
there drowned. Rescue operations were almost impossible in the total darkness caused by the dust cloud.

Thousands of ships were capsized and sunk by the
tsunamis. One, luckier than most, was a Dutch war ship,
the *Beroun*. Anchored in a harbor in Sumatra, she was
picked up by the wave and carried up a river valley for
almost two miles. Today her abandoned hulk lies there,
30 feet above the level of the distant ocean.

Where the sea waves did not strike a beach, they continued to travel, gradually losing their strength. Ships
in the harbor at Port Elizabeth, in South Africa, bobbed
up and down slightly in response to the mighty explosion that had occurred over 5000 miles away. And
careful measurements in the English Channel, halfway

around the world from Krakatoa, showed the last breath of the tremendous tsunamis.

So, Krakatoa was dead, along with about 37,000 people who drowned as a result of its final struggle. But the weakness in the crust of the earth still lies under the Sunda Strait. And the rocks deep in the earth under this weak spot remain hot. Occasionally, the pressure becomes so great it makes the earth shake, and the lava flows quietly forth. On January 25, 1925, a new Krakatoa was born as a tiny island pushed a few feet above the surface of the sea. This volcanic cone, named *Anak Krakatoa*—the "child of Krakatoa"—continues to grow. Sometimes it grows slowly and gradually, and sometimes it grows suddenly and violently. In October of 1952, the island reared upward another 200 feet and now stands at an altitude of over 325 feet above the sea. It seems unlikely that the world has heard the last of Krakatoa or of the destruction that we know this volcano can produce.

CHAPTER TWO

THE CITY PEOPLE FORGOT

IT WAS THE SUMMER of the year 79 A.D. For many days there had been earth tremors, but this was not unusual in Pompeii. Gaius, who was twelve years old, was taking a message to his father. It was a hot August day and he had to walk all the way across town. His mind was more on the annoyance he felt at being given a job ordinarily done by a slave than it was on the frequent shaking of the ground beneath his feet.

His mother had insisted this message was too important for a slave to carry. Besides, the slaves were upset. A huge cloud seemed to be coming out of the tall mountain that stood above the Pompeian scenery. They felt it was a bad omen. The gods must be angry. The women wailed as they hovered inside their quarters.

The fear that gripped them seemed to be in the air. You could almost touch it. Gaius' younger sister held to her mother's skirts all morning. Even his mother, who usually ran her household calmly and efficiently was not herself today. She tried to hide her nervousness, but nevertheless she spoke sharply to Gaius when he complained about having to bear messages like a slave.

At least he would behave like a nobleman, he told himself. He was almost old enough to be considered a man, and he congratulated himself on the fact that he was not afraid. His father had reassured them just that morning that there was nothing to fear.

As Gaius walked through the forum, where the towns-people often gathered to hear politicians speak, he could see the mountain towering 10,000 feet above the marble columns outside the temples. It was about five miles away, but today it seemed much closer. The cloud was very strange looking, he thought. It looked like it came right out of the mountain top and went straight up—just like one of the marble pillars holding up the roof of the Temple of Apollo. Then, at a great height, it billowed out. It reminded him of the trunk and spreading branches of the trees that grew on the mountainside.

His eyes traveled from the cloud down the sides of the mountain. It was green everywhere, the mountain was covered with pine trees and shrubs. Here and there he could see the carefully tended vineyards. The grapes were ripe and sweet this time of year. He was comforted by the sight of those peaceful, luxurious fields and went on his way.

Pompeii was a busy, prosperous city in 79 A.D. As Gaius walked through the city he passed a bakery where grain was ground into flour and bread was made. The wonderful smell of fresh-baked bread reached him, and he inhaled deeply. It made him feel hungry even though he had just finished his mid-day meal. The many shops of the market area were closed during this hot part of the day. The craftsmen who made wool, glass, and items of silver and bronze were quiet. On the walls were painted slogans for the coming elections.

Many of the walls showed signs of damage done by an earthquake that had shaken Pompeii seventeen years earlier. Of course, that was before Gaius was born, but he had heard his father's friends speak of it; there was even a temple to the gods on the forum square, built to show that the people were sorry for whatever wrongs they had committed to bring on such a terrible thing.

They had no way of knowing there was a connection between the now frequent movement of the earth beneath their feet and the cloud growing above the mountain on the horizon. There was no record of Mount Vesuvius having erupted in the past. But the people of Pompeii grew more and more anxious as they watched the cloud turn a dark color.

Gaius walked a little faster and tried not to think about the darkening cloud. Instead he turned his mind to the games that were to take place soon in the amphitheater. As soon as the crops were all in, there would be a big celebration. His thoughts were interrupted by the sight of his father coming out of the house where the thermal baths were. Wealthy Pompeians enjoyed

*Studying such ruins
as these baths
helps us
to understand
how people lived
in 79 A.D. in Pompeii.*

these warm pools of water and often relaxed and talked with their friends while bathing there. His father was talking earnestly with some other men, and Gaius fell in step with them, knowing that he must not interrupt their conversation.

As they walked along, his father put his hand on the boy's shoulder. Gaius felt proud to be considered grown-up enough to be a part of their group. After a few minutes, Gaius' father asked what brought him out in the heat of the day, and Gaius guiltily remembered the message from his mother.

She wanted his father to come home as soon as he could. Gaius told his father the slaves were frightened by the newly formed cloud over the mountain. They were not able to do their work because they felt the gods were angry. They were afraid they were going to be punished for some unknown sins they had committed.

Gaius' father looked up at the cloud with a frown. It had now grown to such a size that it was between them and the sun. There seemed to be occasional bits of something in the air, something that looked like ashes. But there were no fires in Pompeii this time of day in the summer.

As they left the other men and started toward home, the sky became darker and a brisk wind brought larger pieces of ash and fine particles of dirt and sand into the air around them. Some of the bits of sand were really too large to be called sand. They were more like very tiny rocks. From the direction of the mountain, sounds that resembled rolls of thunder became louder and louder. Through the thick clouds Gaius could see enormous streaks of lightning above Vesuvius.

It seemed to Gaius a strange kind of storm, and he gripped his father's hand a little tighter. They reached their house by pushing their way through the small groups of people who now clogged the narrow walkways. Chariots being pulled through the streets were unable to get by the quickly gathering crowds.

Gaius noticed as they went in the door that his mother's usually calm, peaceful face was tense as she greeted them. He felt shocked when he realized she had been crying. There were sounds of wailing from the servants' quarters and his younger sister was sobbing in her mother's arms, while the other sister clung to her skirts.

He listened to his father's calm voice and felt his sagging spirits rise as his father suggested they close the doors and windows to keep out the dust and dirt. His mother remembered the earthquake of 17 years before and suggested they stand out in the courtyard, where nothing could fall on them. But as they stepped out the door, they were caught in a rain of ashes and small stones. They couldn't stay out there. Besides, the air was heavy with a disagreeable smell that made it hard to breathe. Although it was still afternoon, it was almost dark outside.

As they closed the windows, they saw people moving through the streets toward the gates of the city. They were leaving the city, carrying packs of belongings. Some shielded their heads from the falling stones with pillows. Frantically they pushed past one another. They were leaving, but where could they go?

The servants entered the house in a group, and one of them stepped forward. He was a man older than Gaius' father and had been chosen as the spokesman. His hands trembled, and he could not control his voice as he implored the head of the house to take them out of the city, and far away from this terrible thing that was happening.

Gaius' father placed his hand on the old man's arm and spoke to him gently. He explained that there was nowhere to go outside the city walls. The closest city was Herculaneum, and it lay toward the mountain. In the other direction lay the sea. He felt they would be safer there, in the house. He said that fortune favored those who were brave. However, if the slaves wanted to leave, he would not stop them.

The slaves gathered together in a corner. After talking it over, all left except the old man, his wife, and grown daughter. They stayed inside with Gaius and his family while the rest quickly collected a few things and pushed their way through the streets toward the gates.

After most of their servants had fled Pompeii, Gaius' father gathered his family around him, including the old slave and his family. He spoke to them kindly and calmly. He reminded them that they had felt many earth shocks before, some of which were very destructive, but they had all survived them. He admitted that the falling dust, ashes, and stones were dangerous and the vapors in the air were disagreeable to smell, but he asked them to try to ignore these things. He suggested they have their dinner as normally as possible and then go to bed. Tomorrow it would surely all be over.

Gaius admired his father's courage and vowed to try to imitate it. He even played a game with his younger sisters—something he ordinarily would never do. His father sat down to read and his mother supervised the slaves in getting their evening meal ready.

The earth continued to shake. It seemed to Gaius, as he got ready for bed, that the shocks were stronger than ever. He wished they would quit. His father had said he would move the children's cots into their parents' room for the night. Although Gaius wouldn't admit it, even to himself, he felt better about going to bed in their room.

Outside, the ashes continued to fall, like snow. There was also a rain of tiny porous stones, lighter than most rocks. These pumice stones contained many air pockets and even though they were cooler than when hurled from the volcano, they were still too warm to touch. This cloud of ash and dust that covered Pompeii made it impossible to see even an outline of the huge mountain. Where they should have been able to see the top of the mountain, there was a red glow, like flames shooting up. Over the glow, the lightning snapped—more lightning than anyone had ever seen before in one place. It continued all night. The smell of sulfur was so strong in the city that it was more than just disagreeable. It was becoming difficult to breathe.

Gaius felt a hand on his shoulder and heard his father speak his name. He sat up suddenly, his heart beating faster. He heard the others moving about the room, but could hardly see them even though the lamp glowed softly on the table. The cloud outside seemed to have moved into the room with them. His father told him to get dressed. They would have to leave the city. His father gave no sign to the rest of the family of his fears that perhaps they were leaving too late.

The outside door was difficult to open because so much debris had piled against it. Once outside, they made their way through the crowds of people to the gate. Though it was dawn elsewhere in Italy, it was dark in Pompeii. People still pushed their way toward the gates, burdened with bundles of things they felt they couldn't leave behind. Like those who had left the evening before, some tied pillows on their heads to protect them from the falling stones. Others held pieces of tile or cloth over their heads. Everywhere was the sound of wailing and weeping. Mothers called their children. Old men called to their gods. Some feared it was the last eternal night on earth and there were no longer any gods to hear them.

Gaius and his family and slaves kept close together as they went through the streets. Once outside the gates, his father told them to get off the road so they wouldn't be trampled by the crowds. They were to walk through the fields, away from the lightning, which was all they could now see of Vesuvius. His father told them they must keep walking. They were not to sit down even if they were tired. The ashes were getting deep and walking was difficult. Breathing was also difficult and Gaius held one hand in front of his nose and mouth to keep out the ashes. He felt very sleepy. The darkness that was around him was not one of a moonless night. To him it was more like being in a room with no doors or windows.

The next day it began to get light, little by little. It was not like normal daylight, but rather like an eclipse of the sun. The air was full of mist and dust. The ground —indeed the entire city—was covered completely as if by a fresh, very deep snowfall. There were no trees to be seen—not even a building was in sight. All was completely covered. There was no movement anywhere. There was no sound.

As the mist rolled out to sea and the dust settled, Vesuvius looked over the place where the city had been. Vesuvius, which had two days ago been more than 10,000 feet tall, was now less than 4000 feet above sea level. The top 6000 feet of the mountain had been pulverized and blown across the countryside. Pompeii lay under 23 feet of ashes, dust and small stones. Three quarters of her people—approximately 15,000 people—lay buried with her.

Pompeii and her people were mourned by the entire country. A man known as Pliny the Younger wrote two letters describing what he had seen and felt from a nearby city. Martialis and Statius wrote sad poems about the disaster. Then everyone forgot Pompeii. Seeds blew in by the wind and were carried in by birds. Over the years, the ground covering Pompeii became a wilderness. No traces of the city were found, or even looked for, until about the year 1595 when Domenico Fontana made an underground aqueduct to carry water across that part of Italy. His aqueduct ran through a part of old Pompeii, but he was an engineer, not interested in archeology. The statues and vases he found did not lead to further searching.

Occasionally someone digging there found an object of interest and took it away, but it was almost like grave robbing. No scientific digging and restoring of the city was begun until 1748. Slowly, and with few interruptions, it has continued ever since.

Even today the work goes on. It is a job that must be done carefully to prevent the buildings and their contents from being damaged. The city covers an area of 161 acres—161 acres covered by more than 20 feet of volcanic ash that must be removed almost a spoonful at a time.

The rewards for this careful, time-consuming work are great, though. Today you can walk through the streets of the excavated parts of Pompeii. You can walk on the same paving stones the Pompeians walked on. You can examine the ruts that were worn in the stones by chariot wheels.

Walls of houses are still standing, complete with the pictures the Pompeians painted on them. The intricate designs of the mosaic floors are there to please anyone who looks. In the gardens are pools and fountains.

The walls along the streets are painted in red with the names and qualifications of men hoping to be elected to public office. Bread was found in the ovens at the bakery, wine in the wine cellars. Everywhere there are signs of the life of this once-forgotten city.

There is an outdoor theater and a smaller theater once used for music recitals. You can see the gladiators' barracks, the amphitheater for sports events, and the forum where political speeches were made.

The ash and dust, when rained upon, formed a somewhat hardened crust around the bodies of the people who died with Pompeii. The bodies have mostly disintegrated during all of these years, but the hardened ashes of Vesuvius have kept a record of their shape, even their clothes and sometimes the expressions on their faces. By a special process, the molds of some of these bodies have been filled with plaster and allowed to dry. When the mold is chipped away, there is a plaster statue that shows the outline of the person who was there. Even figures of animals have been re-formed in this way. Sometimes a group of figures is found together. One such group was found outside the walls of Pompeii. A boy and a younger girl lie side by side, as if asleep. A short distance away is a woman with a small child close to her. Behind all of them is a grown man, in a half-sitting position, as if he were trying to get up.

There have been other eruptions since Pompeii was buried in 79 A.D., but none so disasterous. For almost 1000 years after that date Vesuvius had minor up-heavals, throwing out small amounts of solid fragments.

This is the usual way that an old, worn out volcano behaves. When it first begins, it sends out lava flows—molten rock that slithers out of the top or from cracks in the sides of the mountain.

As the lava hardens, it "tightens the lid" on the mountain. Not until great force is built up inside the mountain by the expanding gases does it blow off the top again. In the case of Vesuvius, this enormous explosion blew away the top two-thirds of the mountain. Later come smaller and smaller explosions until no more are heard. A volcano is said to be extinct when no more activity is observed for a long period of time.

Then, in the year 1036, a change took place in Vesuvius as new lava began to ooze from the mountain. It had entered a "second childhood." It was rejuvenated. Every few years a new lava flow was seen. In 1904 and again in 1905, lava came out of splits in the sides of

*The 1944 eruption
of Mt. Vesuvius
filled the southern Italian sky,
a reminder of how the city of Pompeii
was buried more than
eighteen centuries earlier.*

the mountain. On April 4, 5, and 6, 1906, new lava mouths opened along the southern side of the mountain. Lava was first seen coming out of a place 500 feet below the top, then from another 1300 feet lower, and finally from another slit 600 feet lower still. These flows were not floods of lava, but were slow-moving. They were still destructive. Fields and houses were damaged. On April 7, a column of steam lifted dust particles four miles straight up from the crater. The cloud was laced with crackles of lightning. Ashes fell on the nearby village of Boscotricano, collapsing roofs. For two weeks the explosions inside the mountain could be heard. Gradually the mountain became quiet.

It has been heard from occasionally since then, but no real damage has been done. In 1944, when the battles of World War II were dotted over Europe, Vesuvius again exploded, and poured out more lava, dust and ash. The Germans and Americans had just been fighting in that area and the battle line was now only 70 miles away. At Naples, an American photographer took pictures of the cloud over Vesuvius.

There was only one man left to attend to the observatory on the side of Mount Vesuvius. Imagine his disappointment that the misfortunes of war had made it impossible to get film for his cameras. The only close-hand records were from the observatory's scientific instruments and his own written words.

The observatory still records seventy to eighty shocks a day from Vesuvius. Most of them are too small to be felt by a person. But if you go up to the top of the mountain and down a little way into the crater, you can place your hand on the sides of the crater and feel its warmth. If you blow your breath against the warm rocks there, the moisture from your breath will cause a small puff of steam to rise. And in the imaginative mind, there will be no doubt that Vulcan, the Greek god of fire, lies sleeping beneath Vesuvius.

CHAPTER THREE

THE GLOWING CLOUD OF DEATH

SOME VOLCANOES, such as Krakatoa and Vesuvius, explode violently when the pressure within them becomes too great. But not all volcanoes throw huge rocks and melted lava into the air. Mount Pelée, perhaps the most deadly killer-volcano of all, caused the death of almost all of the inhabitants of the town of Saint Pierre in an entirely different way.

Across the mouth of the Caribbean Sea, separating it from the Atlantic Ocean, is scattered a 2000-mile-long chain of islands known as the West Indies. The northern-most links in this chain, off the coast of Florida, are the Bahama Islands and Cuba. Near the southern end, some 300 miles from the coast of Venezuela, lies the tiny island of Martinique.

It was the morning of May 8, 1902. Auguste Ciparis lay on his hard bed as the dawn pushed away the shadows in his tiny room. Normally, this would have been a happy season for the young man. Ships were coming regularly to the port of Saint Pierre, and Ciparis had a good job at the docks. He helped to unload the exotic cargo from these ships and reload them with familiar goods that would be taken to far away places.

He had spent his life in the narrow, twisting streets of this pretty little town, which the French rulers called "The Paris of the West Indies." He had always loved to wander through the forests that grew thickly up the sides of the mountain that stood a few miles to the northeast of the city.

"If I were not here," he thought to himself, "what would I do today?"

Perhaps, after receiving his pay, he would have climbed part way up the side of the 4400-foot-high Mount Pelée with a group of friends. There they might sit and watch the setting sun glint off the red tile roofs of the town below them. Or perhaps they would watch the blue water of the Caribbean wash in against the white sand of the two-mile-long beach that separated the town from the water.

"Or perhaps," he thought, "if I were not here, I might even take some food and climb higher up the mountain alone."

There he could have spent the long evening roaming through the tropical forest, following one deep ravine and then another, until he reached the large lake that lay at the very top of the mountain.

But, as the sun rose from the Atlantic Ocean, Ciparis told himself that he would never again explore the sides of Mount Pelée or visit the lake that lay in the crater of the dead volcano. As his tiny room became lighter and lighter with the coming dawn he thought, "No, never again will I climb the mountain."

For Auguste Ciparis had been convicted of murder. His room was a tiny cell in the city jail, a solid room without a window through which he could look at the bustle of Saint Pierre. It was here he waited for the day of his execution.

He got up from his hard bed and stood by the tiny, barred window in the iron door, which was the only source of fresh air. He waited for his jailer to bring his breakfast and news of the 35,000 people who lived in freedom just beyond the walls. From where he stood he could see, far down the dark passageway, the light of coming day.

Suddenly, the light disappeared, as if a heavy cloud had covered the sun, and a blast of hot air flowed through the tiny window. As he fell back, the heat grew and grew. He could not escape it. Screaming from the burning pain, Ciparis rolled on the floor and finally under his bed, where he fainted.

Later that day, he regained consciousness. Even though his clothing was not burned, his flesh was badly scorched. Fortunately, he had protected his face by burying it in his arms. Again and again he called for help. But no one came. Hour after long hour he lay, watching his burned flesh darken and erupt into open sores. Without food or water, and in constant pain, he waited for death to come.

But he did not die. After four days of pain and suffering, he heard the sound of voices! From his bed, he called and called until, at last, faces appeared at the barred window. He was rescued!

After a welcome drink of water, Ciparis limped from his prison and into the daylight that he thought he would never see again. As he painfully hobbled along, leaning heavily on the shoulders of one of his rescuers, he stared around him in amazement. The once-busy port of Saint Pierre was gone! Only the broken stone walls of its many houses were to be seen. The only people he could see were strangers, rescue teams from neighboring towns. Of the 38,000 townspeople and visitors who had been in Saint Pierre on the morning of May 8, only Ciparis and one other man had managed to survive.

Most of the people who had lived in the city had known that Mount Pelée was a volcano, of course, but its last eruption had been over 50 years before, and that had been a very minor one. At that time, in 1851, both the large crater at the very top of the mountain and the smaller one along the side had been filled with water, forming two very pretty crater lakes. After minor earthquakes, the smaller lake had disappeared, apparently evaporated by heat from below. The eruption that followed was so small that only a few ashes blew down into the town, and for a few days white clouds of steam drifted over the mountain.

Since then, the mountain had remained quiet. That is, everything seemed quiet until May, 1901, when a group of people journeyed to the dry lake bed to have a picnic. There they found a small jet of steam coming from the ground. When they returned to the city, they reported that their favorite picnic spot had been spoiled forever. The smell of sulfur, they said, was terrible, and all of the beautiful forests around the crater had been killed. But, for almost a year, nothing else happened, and the people of Saint Pierre soon found other spots for their picnics.

Then, in late April, 1902, three small explosions were heard—and felt—in the city. These small earthquakes did no damage, and caused little worry. But the next day a tall column of steam and ash was seen rising from the small crater on the side of the mountain, clouding the crest of the upper peak with a cap of white vapor. A group of scientists from the local university climbed to the peak and, looking down into the crater half-way down the slope, saw that it was rapidly filling with boiling black water that gave off a strong smell of sulfur. Investigating further, they discovered a small cone about 30 feet high that had formed near the edge of the old lake bed. From it spewed a constant stream of steam and ash.

With the coming of May, the earthquakes began again. And beginning with the morning of May 2, white ash and black cinders began to shower down on Saint Pierre. About midnight that night, the townspeople were shaken from their beds by the noise of tremendous explosions. Rushing into the streets, they looked toward the mountain. Even in the darkness they could see a column of smoke, black even against the night sky. Flashes of lightning played throughout the cloud, and the noise became louder and louder still. The fall of ash was reported from every part of the island.

Saturday, the third of May, was a busy day in Saint Pierre. The dust, as fine as flour, sifted through tiny cracks into the most tightly closed houses, and the women spent most of their time sweeping. The red-tiled roofs were covered by a thin coating of the ash, and the people of the city stayed in their homes as much as possible. Even with their doors and windows shut, their throats became sore and their eyes red from the irritating dust. The local newspaper reported on that day, "The cinder rain never stops."

Why didn't the people of Saint Pierre desert their town now? Surely they realized that Mount Pelée was in full eruption, and the town was threatened. It is difficult to say, but perhaps the reason the town waited too long was that an election was to be held in just one week. From the newspaper reports, it seems as if the government was afraid to order the evacuation of the threatened cities and villages for fear of upsetting the plans for the election. Whatever the cause, the townspeople waited too long.

Those brave men who dared leave the safety of their homes and visit the forest reported that all of the wild animals had left the mountainside. Even the birds refused to sing. Did they, somehow, know that disaster was coming? Or perhaps the darkness that had closed in over the little island made them think it was night.

Slowly, that strange Saturday came to an end. No farmers came to the city to sell their vegetables, for their horses refused to move through the falling fog of ash. The water in the harbor turned black with the dust that fell into it. All of the schools and colleges closed, and the students were sent home. Many businesses closed and all unnecessary traffic was forbidden. As the people huddled in their homes, faces wrapped with damp cloths in an attempt to filter out ash from the air they breathed, they could not hear the wheels of the fire wagons that were constantly watering down the dusty streets. All noise, even the sound of the wheels of the heavy carriages, was muffled by the thick dust that now covered the streets from house to house. Outside the town, birds and cattle began to die, some of starvation because the dust covered the trees and grass with a thick coating, others of suffocation as the fine ash found its way into their lungs.

North of Saint Pierre lay a stream called the Rivière Blanche—the "white river." Under more normal conditions, it foamed with a milky whiteness as it rushed down the side of Mount Pelée. Now, in spite of the lack of rain along the coast, the little river became a black torrent. It rolled huge rocks before it, and carried tree trunks along in its muddy water. This increase in flow came, apparently, from the large amounts of steam that had risen into the air from the volcano. This steam, rising high above the island, cooled and condensed into rain.

It was the rain falling high above on the mountain's side that claimed the first human lives. About noon on May 5, the people of Saint Pierre saw a new column of what they thought was steam, coming from the side of the mountain. They thought that perhaps a new vent had opened, but this idea turned out to be wrong.

As the water from the rains high on the mountain rushed down the ravines, it was first blocked by the heavy ash. Then, after several large ponds had formed, the water broke loose and washed down the slope. The nearly boiling water gave off clouds of steam as it came. Moving at nearly 60 miles an hour down the mountain, the water picked up and carried along with it tons of ash and rock. Described by one eye-witness as a "rolling mountain," the avalanche passed over a sugar mill, burying its owner, his wife, and 40 workers beneath many feet of mud and rock. But now only the very top of the smokestack of the mill was left to mark the grave of its workers.

Within a few minutes, the wall of mud and rock reached the ocean along the west coast of the island. The wave forced upward by the force of the mud flow struck the anchored yacht *Pecheur* in the side and turned her over. So sudden was this disaster that not a single member of the crew managed to escape drowning. The wave then reversed directions and flung itself into the harbor of Saint Pierre. As it did so, it flooded many of the town's low-lying streets.

The knowledge that living close to Mount Pelée was dangerous caused the people of the city that lay at its base to be frightened. Many began to make ready to leave the island. The American government sent a schooner into the harbor for the purpose of removing from the island any American citizen who wished to leave. Feeling that the large city would be the safest place to be, about 3500 people moved from the sides of the mountain into the doomed Saint Pierre. The empty schools were used by many of these refugees as places to live until they could return home.

On May 7, the explosions increased in violence. These muffled booms blended with the crack of thunder and the constant lion-like roars of the crater itself. Even in the daylight a glow could be seen coming from the crater at the top of Mount Pelée. Marino Leboffee, Captain of the Italian ship *Orsolina*, looked at the glowing cloud above the mountain and announced that he was leaving immediately, in spite of the fact that his ship was only half loaded. "I have seen Vesuvius," he told his friends. "If she ever looked like that, I would leave as quickly as I could."

The *Orsolina* slowly made its way through the harbor, its water black with ash and clogged with tree trunks, floating pumice rocks, and the bodies of dead animals. As the ship safely cleared the harbor mouth, the wind shifted suddenly and for the first time in almost a week, the air above the city began to clear.

The next morning dawned clear and warm. The people of Saint Pierre streamed out into the welcome sunshine, hardly glancing at the tall column of dark smoke that rose from the very top of the nearby mountain. The bells of the church tower tolled, announcing the dawn of Ascension Day, the 40th morning after Easter. In the harbor, 18 ships rode quietly at anchor. The hands of the church clock showed 13 minutes to 8. At 7:50 a.m., they stopped forever.

Deep within the mountain, gases had been escaping from the melted rock. Since the path to the surface was closed except for a small vent through which the steam and ash were escaping, the pressure built higher and higher. By 7:47 a.m. on May 8, the pressure had built up to the point that it was strong enough to break through to the outside. Unfortunately for Saint Pierre and her inhabitants, the gases did not push the lava in the crater out in an explosion similar to those of Vesuvius and Krakatoa. Since the weakest place on the mountain lay along its side, above Saint Pierre, a huge crack appeared there, well below the lava plug.

From this fissure rushed a glowing cloud, made of gas and glowing solid particles. The material making up the superheated cloud was heavier than the air. It hugged the ground and flowed like water down the slope toward the town. Moving at a speed that must have been very close to 200 miles per hour, the glowing cloud rushed through Saint Pierre and into the harbor. Everything touched by the blast was charred, not catching fire because the cloud did not contain any oxygen. After the cloud passed, the oxygen from the air came into contact with the superheated town and the fires began.

When the glowing cloud reached the harbor it caused destruction almost as complete as that created in the city. Of the 18 ships there, only the British steamship *Roddam* managed to escape, with the loss of half of the people on board. Around the *Roddam*, other ships capsized and sank. Masts, smokestacks—everything above the decks—were swept away, leaving only charred, shriveled debris. Where the glowing cloud touched the water, huge columns of steam rose from the boiling surface.

Later that afternoon, the first team of rescuers reached Saint Pierre. They found that a ten-square-mile area had been completely destroyed. With the exception of Auguste Ciparis, the murderer, and one other man, all life in the area had been wiped out. They found the harbor clogged with overturned and burning boats and unidentifiable wreckage. Along the docks, piles of lumber burned brightly, as did smaller fires scattered throughout the town and on the hills outside. They found iron

The clouds of Mt. Pelée, a volcano on Martinique, rise above the outskirts of Saint Pierre's harbor.

bars that had been twisted by the heat, and walls that had been knocked down by the force of the blast. Wooden timbers, apparently somewhat protected, had turned to charcoal. The destruction of Saint Pierre was so complete that when, on May 20, another glowing cloud again burst forth from the fissure in the side of Mount Pelée, it passed right through the town, but no new damage was reported.

Three months later, the glowing cloud again appeared. But this time it took a slightly different direction. Sweeping down the eastern slope of the mountain, this glowing cloud destroyed five small villages and killed about 2000 people.

The glowing cloud of death from Mount Pelée and those of several other volcanoes is caused by the same conditions that cause the violent explosions of moun-

tains like Krakatoa and Vesuvius. The lava from volcanoes like Mount Pelée is more solid than liquid, in
spite of its high temperature. Since it is not very liquid,
the gases in it cannot escape easily, and the pressure
builds up until these gases finally escape violently—by
blowing the material away.

This appears to be especially true of volcanoes like
Mount Pelée. Almost a half a year after the destruction
of Saint Pierre, an almost solid plug was pushed upward
from the crater of the mountain. Up and up it came, so
nearly solid that it held its shape—a cylinder almost
500 feet thick. It rose at a rate of 30 feet a day until it
stood over 1000 feet above the rim of the crater. At first,
this spine of lava was so hot that it glowed, and was easily
seen from the sea at night. Slowly, it began to cool and
its surface broke into huge chunks that fell back into the
crater. At last, several months later, it collapsed completely, and Mount Pelée again became quiet.

And so it remained until 1929. At that time it seemed
that the mountain might repeat its performance of almost 30 years before, but this time the people of the
island knew what Mount Pelée could do. As soon as the
flow of ash began, the island was evacuated. A few small
glowing clouds and one large one appeared, but they
caused little damage and no loss of life. Spines of lava
appeared several years later, but none so large as the one
that stood over the ruins of Saint Pierre in 1902. No new
glowing clouds have been formed, but the people of the
new Saint Pierre know how deadly their neighboring
mountain can be. They live with the feeling that Mount
Pelée is only sleeping, gathering its strength for another
attack on the people of Martinique.

CHAPTER FOUR

THE "MUDDY CLOUD" OF TAAL

SUPPOSE YOU KNEW that a certain volcano had erupted at least 18 times in the last 400 years—an average of once every 22 years. It had killed perhaps half of the people who had lived near it. Would you want to build your house at its base? Probably not, but amazingly that is exactly what the people on the southern end of the island of Luzon do!

Luzon is the largest and most important of the more than 7000 Philippine islands. Almost three million people live in Manila and neighboring Quezon City, the national capital. Just 40 miles south of these cities there is a rather large lake named Bombon. In the center of this lake is a killer volcano named Taal.

Throughout the long written history of the Philippines, Taal has proven itself to be a deadly neighbor for the villagers living near it. As early as 1572, one year after the city of Manila was founded, a Spanish priest established a village on the shore of Lake Bombon. At that time, he wrote that the Taal mountain "spits forth many large rocks, which destroy the crops of the natives."

During the next 200 years after this first written record, Taal erupted an even dozen times. Many houses and a great number of crops were destroyed by these eruptions, but the loss of life was small. This was probably because the number of people living very close to the volcano was not very great. Then, in 1754, the volcano again began to roar. According to Father Buencuchillo, the priest living at the village of Taal, the explosions "threw sky-high flames, mixed with glowing rocks." These hot rocks rolled down the sides of the volcano, making it look as if the mountain was cut by rivers of fire. This eruption began on May 15, lasted all summer, and continued through the night of September 25— there were almost 17 weeks of continuous noise, smoke, and flying rocks!

The night of September 25 was a particularly bad one, and when the dim sun finally showed feebly through the haze, Father Buencuchillo took a brief walk through his village. He found an 18-inch covering of ash everywhere. Not only were the plants growing in the fields crushed by the weight of the ash, but the roofs of many houses were also sagging dangerously. Though the volcano was now quieter, the priest ordered the villagers to leave Taal.

With his people safely away from the danger, Father Buencuchillo returned to the village with a small group of men to watch over the property of the Church. During the night of November 1, the mountain again became fierce. The priest estimated that during this one night the volcano "ejected fire, rock, sand, and mud in greater quantities than ever before." By November 15, explosions forced huge rocks over the rim of the crater. They rolled down the slopes and into the water of the lake. The waves caused by these boulders were large enough to wash over the lowest land around the lake. The ground shook and swayed, and houses tottered dangerously. By this time, everyone in the area had moved to what they hoped was a safe distance away. Everyone had moved, that is, with the exception of the brave Father Buencuchillo. Because of his courage, we know what happened during the next few weeks.

The volcano continued to roar, throwing out a constant stream of ash, cinders, and large rocks. Late in the evening of November 28, the mountain suddenly seemed to gain strength. It belched out a huge quantity of ash and mud that was caught up in a towering, cauliflower-shaped cloud. The priest, standing in his damaged church building, watched the cloud. Beneath it the island was shrouded in drifting clouds of black ash. Glowing hot rocks continually rolled down its flanks. Lightning lit the darkened sky above him, while earthquakes shook the ground beneath his feet. For some reason not yet understood, the water of the lake suddenly rose, flooding what was left of the village of Taal. As the water became deeper and deeper, Father Buencuchillo unwillingly abandoned his church and stumbled through the dark jungle until he reached a low hill a mile and a half farther away from the erupting volcano.

As the priest huddled in the darkness, the volcano suddenly became quiet. In some ways, the stillness was more frightening than the constant noise. The next morning the sun came up above the horizon, brightly shining on the destruction below. Quickly, Father Buencuchillo hurried back to his church. As he dug through the mixture of mud and ashes that had buried his holy objects, smoke again spouted from the mouth of the crater. As the thunderous crashes from the volcano became louder and louder, the priest abandoned his church and village once more.

This time, he took his belongings to the church in the town of Caysasay, 12 miles inland. But the priest was not to escape the wrath of Taal by simply moving a few miles. By 4 o'clock that afternoon, the sky above Caysasay began to grow dark. Soon the air was filled with ash and mud. For three days the sunlight could not reach the ground, and the people of Caysasay worked steadily to clean the rapidly gathering ash from the roof of the church. Throughout the 72 hours of darkness, they worked. Their only light was the huge lightning bolts that constantly flashed above them, for the damp ash smothered candles and lanterns almost as quickly as they were lighted. Father Buencuchillo and his fellow priests spent the night of November 30 huddled together on the inside stairway of the church—a spot hopefully protected from falling roofs. Throughout the night they sat and listened to the crash of houses collapsing around them. Just before daylight, on the first of December, the weight of the ash that had accumulated on the church became too great for the structure and a part of the roof gave way.

A few hours later, the frightened people of Caysasay discovered that daylight was returning. As the sun shown redly through the dusty air, they looked at what was left of their town. Father Buencuchillo, unhurt by the fall of the church roof, later estimated that the ashes lay more than three and a half feet deep over the village!

In the ruins of the village of Taal, the situation was even worse. Seven and a half feet of ash buried everything but a few ruined walls of the destroyed church. Even the rivers were buried in mud. With the outlets to the lake blocked, the water slowly crept into the towns around its banks. As they were steadily flooded, the debris washed into the deeper water. All of the animals and plants around the lake were dead, and so were at least a dozen people. Actually, Father Buencuchillo admitted sadly, no one would ever know how many people had died in the eruption that lasted for almost seven months.

(Pages 54–55)
*The clouds of ash
rising from Taal,
in the Philippines,
warn nearby residents
that this volcano still lives!*

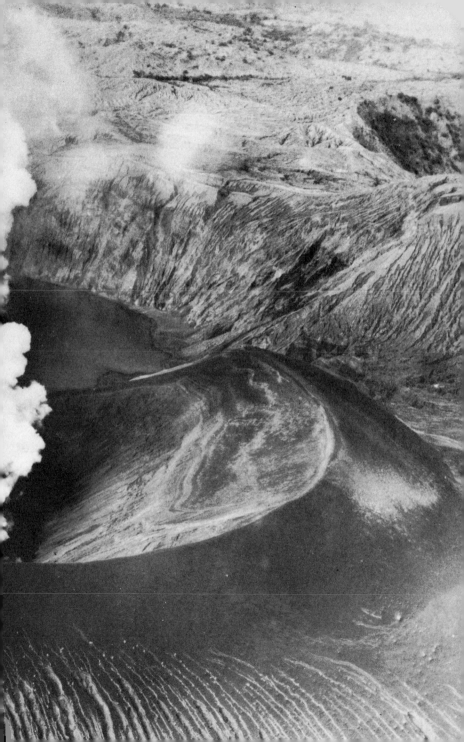

During the next 160 years Taal erupted only four times, without doing much damage. Slowly during this time the trees and other plants found root in the ash, and the people followed the plants back. By 1911, the borders of the lake were again inhabited, and more than 500 people lived on the volcanic island itself.

Up to this time, Taal had acted very much like Mount Vesuvius. It had produced large amounts of ash, which towered above the crater in huge, cauliflower-shaped clouds. It had thrown out large rocks, along with many smaller stones and pebbles.

Over the years, the looks of the volcano had gradually changed. With each eruption, its crater had become larger and larger until, by 1911, it was a caldera almost a mile and a half across. The eastern rim of this caldera was almost 600 feet higher than its western rim.

Inside the caldera were two ponds, called the Yellow Lake and the Green Lake. The Green Lake plays an important role in the story of what happened in 1911. For many years, sulfur gas had bubbled up through its water. Some of this sulfur apparently combined chemically with the water of the lake, forming sulfuric acid. Scientists had not determined that this was actually a natural lake of acid, but the local natives had often reported that the water would "burn" your hands if you put them into it.

The first earthquake shocks were recorded in Manila at 10:20 on the night of January 27, 1911. Like Krakatoa, the Philippines lie above an area where the crust is weak and the forces inside the earth are strong. Since earth-quakes are common here, no one was particularly concerned about them. During the next day, however, more than 200 earthquakes were felt in the city, and word was received that Taal was beginning to throw out rocks, mud, and ash.

A man named Charles Martin was sent to take photographs of the volcano. Martin was, like Father Buencuchillo, a very brave man. As it turned out, he was also a very lucky man.

On the morning of January 29, Martin crossed the lake in a small boat to the steaming volcano. The waters around him were twisting and turning from the movement of the surface of the mountain and the bottom of the lake itself. Arriving at the island, he climbed to the lower western rim. Once there, he took many photographs of the scene below him. They showed three active vents, one being the Green Lake itself. A steady stream of steam boiled up through the peculiar "water," while hot mud and small rocks were thrown up into the air from two nearby cracks in the earth.

Martin had planned to spend the night camping on the slopes of the volcano, but before darkness came he discovered he had used all of his film. Disappointed, the young man returned to the nearby village of Tanauan for the night, where he could get more plates of film. For the first time, fate had stepped in to save his life.

At about one o'clock the next morning, Martin and everyone within 300 miles of Taal were shaken from their beds by a tremendous explosion. Rushing outside, the photographer saw a column of blackness rising high into the sky above the volcano. The cloud was brightly lighted by chains of lightning, which continually ripped through it. Soon, Martin found that he had to find shelter from a heavy rain of mud and ash that showered down on him.

An hour later, at two o'clock on the morning of January 29, a double explosion blasted through the floor of the Taal caldera. The explosion was heard for 600 miles in all directions, and the towering cauliflower-shaped cloud was seen halfway up the island of Luzon— over 250 miles away! In Tanauan village, Martin found himself in total darkness, which would last until noon the next day.

Charles Martin went with the first rescue team to visit the island the next afternoon. He found that, of the more than 500 people who had lived on the side of Taal, only a dozen had lived through the first explosion. These confused and shocked people told him that scalding, burning mud had poured through their palm-thatched houses. Their friends and families had died from breathing the fumes. Each of the survivors was burned over most of his body, but not from burns caused by hot liquids. Instead, they looked more like the burns a strong acid might make!

Martin was busy for the next hour, taking pictures of the destruction. And, again, his luck held. At exactly 3:45 that afternoon, he pushed his little boat away from the island. At four o'clock a final explosion smothered the island with more water from the Green Lake. The water had become a scalding vapor or cloud, heated by the volcano.

A U.S. Army camp was located about six miles from the volcano. One of the men stationed there reported seeing a "cloud of mud" drift over the lower side of the crater rim. The cloud, being heavier than air, flowed down the mountain side, enveloping the villagers below. Then it blew across the little lake toward the camp. A strong wind struck the camp, blowing down tents and flinging men before it. Almost immediately, a tidal wave struck the shore and flooded the camp, which was inshore a quarter of a mile. The American soldiers ran ahead of the mud cloud and finally found a low hill on which they could find shelter.

The muddy cloud swept the western shore of the lake, destroying 13 small villages. In all, almost 2000 people were killed. Some of these victims were buried by the ash and rocks that collapsed the roofs of their houses. But most of the dead were suffocated and burned by the fumes of the cloud of acid.

In the case of four villages, nothing was ever found. The tidal wave that followed the explosion washed ashore, gathered up every house, animal, and person, and washed them back into the lake. The violence of the eruption caused eight-inch-thick trees to break off evenly, about two feet off the ground. The nearby trees that were left standing were stripped of their bark.

No sooner had the rocks of Taal cooled than people again returned to the island. During the next half-century, over 100 people built houses along the slopes of the volcano, and thousands more farmed the land around the edges of the lake.

In August, 1965, wisps of steam began to rise from the lake that then lay in the bottom of the caldera. Scientists visited the lake and discovered that the temperature of the water had increased to 115°F. They joined with friends and relatives in urging the people of the island to move to safer ground, but very few of them followed this advice.

"We cannot leave now," the islanders explained. "Soon the rice must be harvested."

"We will leave at the first earthquake," they promised.

But Taal gave them no warning this time. Instead, suddenly, during the first week of October, a large crack appeared in the southwestern side of the cone, and another muddy cloud appeared. This one traveled only a few miles, snuffing out the lives of the villagers living closest to it.

The pilot of an airliner passed over the volcano a short time later. He radioed a report that the lake in the caldera had turned "as red as a charcoal ember." This "ember" grew and grew, until it had destroyed over 500 people who lived on the western slopes of the mountain. Huge rocks were thrown for more than 12 miles, killing and crippling many people who had believed they were safe so far from the lake.

Although no one can be certain of the number, perhaps 3000 people died because of this eruption of Taal. Not all were killed by the rocks of the muddy cloud. Some were overcome by sulfur fumes that drifted for miles in all directions. Others were killed when their boats capsized in the tormented water of the lake. Still others were killed by their neighbors who, crazed with fear and panic, murdered their friends in order to steal their boats.

Yet people continue to live near the killer Taal. Geologists who have studied the volcano believe that it will erupt again, perhaps at any time. If it does, more people will surely be added to its list of victims.

CHAPTER FIVE

FIRE
AT
SEA!

As OLAFUR VESTMANN walked the deck of the fishing vessel *Isleifur II*, he felt it lurch in an unfamiliar way beneath his feet. It flashed through his mind that it almost felt as if the ship were caught in a whirlpool. But this didn't seem reasonable, so he walked around the deck, searching the Icelandic waters with his eyes.

Although he was the ship's cook, Olafur stood watch that morning because the crew was below deck, resting. They had just finished laying a 12-mile codfish line and they were tired.

Olafur had to concentrate very hard as he looked for what had caused the ship to behave so peculiarly. Although it was almost 7:30, it was barely dawn. It was November 14, 1963, and of course, during the fall the days are very short in Iceland.

As his eyes worked their way farther and farther from the ship, he thought he saw something rise from the sea. He later told the captain it looked like a rock. As he continued to peer through the pre-dawn morning, he realized he saw smoke some distance away. His first thought was that another ship might be on fire, and he went below to wake the skipper.

Captain Gudmar Tomasson agreed that it could be a ship in trouble, and he called the radio station on the nearby Vestmann Islands on his ship-to-shore phone. They reported that they had not received any SOS signals that morning. So Tomasson leaned on the rail, looking at the smoke through the binoculars. He remembered the unpleasant smell he had noticed just before he had gone down to rest. That sulfur smell and the columns of smoke coming out of the sea caused him to suspect there was a volcano erupting under the water.

He called the radio station again, reporting his suspicions, and then ordered the crew to sail toward the pillar of smoke.

Word of the *Isleifur's* sighting quickly reached Dr. Sigurdur Thorarinsson, an Icelandic volcanologist. He was very excited, but not really surprised. After all, Iceland is the largest above-sea portion of the 10,000-mile Mid-Atlantic Ridge. This mostly underwater mountain chain runs from Bouvet in the South Atlantic to Jan Mayen, which lies above the Arctic Circle. Volcanic activity is rather common along this sub-oceanic ridge. Iceland's history is full of reports of volcanoes and earth tremors.

Dr. Thorarinsson arranged for a plane to fly him to the eruption, which was reported to be about 75 miles southeast of Reykjavik, Iceland's capital.

Back on board the *Isleifur*, the skipper got to within half a nautical mile of the eruption. The sea was very rough. As the ship got closer and closer, the churning of the water increased. All of a sudden, the turbulence seemed to move toward the ship. Captain Tomasson ordered a change in the ship's direction. When it was a safe distance away, the ship stopped and the men watched the smoke pillar grow taller. By eight o'clock it was apparent the smoke rose out of the sea at several places and reached a height of about two hundred feet.

On deck, the crew watched motionlessly. The eruptions under the sea were sending higher and higher the smoke and particles of ash, cinders, and pumice, called *tephra*. At ten o'clock the captain decided to head back into the turbulent area. He wanted to study it more closely. He was afraid that if the activity stopped as suddenly as it began, before anyone else arrived, the world might not believe him.

This time the ship got a little closer than it had before. The engineer measured the temperature of the water and found it to be 54.5° F, about nine Fahrenheit degrees higher than normal for that time of year. The men could see stones being thrown out of the sea, and flashes of light streaked through the towers of tephra. But so far, there seemed to be no noticeable noise coming from the upheaval.

At about eleven o'clock, Dr. Thorarinsson's plane flew over the volcano. The pillars of steam and tephra had by that time climbed to 12,000 feet. The water was a brownish-green color, in sharp contrast to the turquoise water all around.

By three o'clock the evidence of this eruption stood four miles high and could be seen from Reykjavik. Waves began to break on some unseen barrier below the surface—the birthpangs of a newly forming island.

Just as a nurse watches over a newborn child, Dr. Thorarinsson kept vigil over this infant island. During the next three and a half years he made more than a hundred trips to gather information and see first hand how his "baby" was developing.

What were the forewarnings of this event? They were few, indeed, and none of them was recognized as a sign of a new volcano showing its face. During the three days before the eruption made itself known, the people on one of the Vestmann Islands complained of a sulfur smell. Villagers and farmers went around, looking for the cause of this disagreeable odor, but found none. In the wee hours of the morning of November 13, the trawler *Thorsteinn Thorskabitur* found a sudden rise in the temperature of the water. Another reading was taken, but by this time the ship had passed over the area, and the temperature reading was again normal. The seismographs—earthquake recording instruments—at Reykjavik had registered only weak tremors during the week before, and none at all on November 14.

The ocean floor was about 425 feet below sea level at the place the new island was forming. Dr. Thorarinsson guessed that the eruption had been going on slowly for some days before it came to the surface. An underwater mountain was building up. It was made up of the loose, porous material formed when the hot lava of the volcano met the cold sea water. Only when this mountain grew taller than the surface of the sea did the world realize what was happening.

Daylight of the next morning, November 15, found this fledgling island to be 33 feet high and still growing. By November 19 it was 200 feet high and 2000 feet long. The cloud that spouted out of it reached a height of almost six miles at times. The people of Reykjavik watched it with interest. The Vestmann Islanders dismissed school one day so the children could observe this seldom-seen event.

The inhabitants of the Vestmann Islands viewed this huge cloud as more than just a curiosity, though. They were afraid the northerly winds would bring the airborne ash and pumice over their homes. And it did. The normally sparkling-clean town of Vestmannaeyjar was turned to a gray, sooty, dirty-looking place. The islanders' only supply of fresh water is rain that is collected from roof tops. Since a quarter inch of volcanic ash covered their roofs, the people were worried about their water supply. They were afraid it would be dangerous to drink because of the high fluorine content of the ash. And the sulfur left it with a disagreeable smell. The problem was solved by rinsing the roofs with sea water pumped through fire hoses. Then the next rain fell on clean roofs.

The men of Vestmannaeyjar worried about the effect of the eruption on their fishing. Cod fishing is the main source of income for the town. But a few days later the catches were excellent and the men felt relieved. Even the farmers benefited. The fields were greener that summer than anyone could remember their being in the past.

As the new volcano continued to grow, the Icelandic government's Place Name Committee gave the island a name—*Surtsey*. It was named after the mythological giant Surtur, who brought fire from the south to fight the Icelandic god of fertility, Frey.

Dr. Thorarinsson and others who studied Surtsey feared the island would not last long. Made of loose, dry particles, they felt it would eventually be washed away by the action of the sea waves. The only thing that would save it would be a covering of liquid lava that could harden and withstand the washing of the ocean.

As the days went by, Dr. Thorarinsson recorded Surtsey's progress from planes and boats. When the water got rough, he would be drenched as the boat was washed by waves. But he was caught up in what was taking place. When ocean waves washed into the vents on the top of Surtsey, or when water seeped into the fissure through the porous sides, there would be a loud, rumbling explosion. Then a rush of dark tephra and steam would shoot up, along with huge lumps of liquid or partially congealed lava. These lumps are called *bombs*. Each bomb was followed by a black tail of tephra, looking much like a meteor shooting through the sky. When the hot bombs landed in the cold water, there would be a loud explosion as the difference in temperature caused the bomb to break apart. Then a puff of steam would rise from the spot. Above the island, the column of tephra would be constantly bombarded by lightning and claps of thunder. With all of this to watch, Dr. Thorarinsson almost forgot that he was cold and wet and just a little seasick.

He first set foot on the island on December 16, when he and another scientist landed to collect *xenoliths*—old rocks brought up from beneath the bottom of the ocean by the blasts. They brought back these samples along with some of the new volcanic material to be analyzed. Surtsey was quiet for their short visit, but knowing the activity could begin again at any moment lent an air of suspense to the scene.

The next excursion to Surtsey was not so quiet. On February 19, a group of scientists and volcano enthusiasts boarded the 30-ton motor vessel, *Haraldur*, and sailed for the island. The volcano seemed quiet as they approached, but the water wasn't. Dr. Thorarinsson, four other men, and two women, were drenched as they went ashore in two rubber landing dinghies. The swells against the island were enormous and one dinghy turned over. Some of the equipment was lost, the rest was soaked. Fortunately, no one was hurt.

As they stood dripping on the dark colored sand, the people were grateful that the vent was not erupting. They had only been ashore minutes, however, before they heard loud noises from the volcano and saw water spouts in the water, just off shore. The spouts were splashes from the debris being thrown out of the volcano into the sea. Soon tephra and volcanic bombs began to fall around them. Their first impulse was to run, but where? To be afloat in the rubber raft would be dangerous with hot rocks raining on them. On shore they could dodge the bigger ones. The best thing to do was to stand still and watch the sky, not moving when you saw one coming your way until the last minute. It took a lot of self-control as some of the bombs were three feet across.

Scientists stood on the new volcanic island
of Surtsey as another island came into being.
Unfortunately, the loose tephra of the new island
was never covered with lava
and the waves eventually washed it away.

As the bombs hit the shore, they caused small craters to form. When the waves washed ashore and into these holes in the sand, the water would boil as it touched the hot bombs. This would cause a puff of steam to rise from each crater.

The people on board the *Haraldur* were very concerned about the safety of those on the island. Every time a shower of tephra went up, the island was surrounded by a brownish cloud. This cut off the view of the landing party. As the rain of rocks became heavier, the *Haraldur* had to move farther away from the island.

On the island, no one was injured. They watched for falling bombs, moving out of the way when necessary. The brown pumice grains swirled all around, but they were very light in weight and did not hurt anyone. Between explosions a stiff breeze cleared the air, making it easier to breathe. Eventually the volcano became quieter and the seven people on shore made their way through the heavy surf and rowed the dinghies back to the ship. It was an experience none of them would ever forget. No more attempts were made to go ashore while an explosive vent was still at work.

As the weeks went by, the question was asked over and over again, "Will Surtsey last, or will it be washed away?" The only answer Dr. Thorarinsson could give was that Surtsey was surely doomed unless its surface of loose

tephra was covered by a layer of lava. The lava would harden and keep the island from being washed away by the waves.

They watched anxiously as the crater built up around the vent. Lava could not flow as long as the water could run into the vent through the top or seep in through the loose, porous walls. As soon as the water came in contact with the lava down in the vent, an explosion took place. The lava would be broken up and cooled into ash, cinders, and pumice.

At first the crater took on a horseshoe shape, with the open side toward the north, where the waves kept the tephra washed away. Then the winds shifted, allowing the northern side to build up, along with Dr. Thorarinsson's hopes for a lava flow. But he was disappointed, for now the southerly winds merely tore a hole in the south side of the crater, and only served to change the direction of the horseshoe.

By the end of March, Surtsey was the second largest of the Vestmann Islands, but its life depended on the wind and weather. If they were favorable, a lava pool could build up in the crater. On April 3, an Icelandic coast-guard pilot reported the wall between the vent and the water was wider than ever seen before. Later that night a 500-foot-high fiery red column was reported.

Dr. Thorarinsson again flew over the island on the afternoon of April 4. From above, he saw a glowing lava lake about 400 feet in diameter. The red-hot liquid ran down the sides of the crater, breaking into little rivulets as it spread out on the beach. Each little trickle of lava was greeted at the water's edge by a white puff of steam. The men in the airplane felt they had never seen anything so beautiful. Now Dr. Thorarinsson could answer that often asked question. Surtsey would survive!

For almost a month, lava fountains spouted up, at times more than a hundred feet high. This liquid fire overflowed the crater, forming a shield over more than half the island as it hardened. Those who made night excursions along the water's edge were fascinated by the fiery island.

After the lava ceased to flow, it remained in sight within the crater. It seemed "restless." At times it came up to the rim, at other times it stayed down in the vent. There were breakers in the surface and lava splashed up against the sides of the crater. Gradually, the neck of the vent narrowed as molten rock splattered and hardened on its inner surface.

In early July, the lava began to flow again. At first it overflowed the rim and ran down the sides. Then the top of the lava lake became mostly covered by a scum of partly hardened lava. The lava could still be seen glowing under the surface. The heat from the molten material in the crater evidently melted away portions of the inner walls, and lava found its way through tunnels beneath the surface of the island. Often these tubes did not come to the surface until they were close to the seashore. Some of them undoubtedly extended out under the sea.

The lava continued to flow, and by the end of March, 1965, scientists estimated that the flow was about five cubic yards a second. After that it decreased gradually until July. Then the only activity seemed to be an occasional column of vapor coming up from the vent.

Surtur, as the vent is called, has occasionally shown the world it is not dead by producing more rather un-

spectacular lava flows. But for the most part it "sleeps."
In spite of this dwindling of volcanic activity, the island
has not lost its admirers.

Scientists from all over the world came to a meeting in
Reykjavik in the spring of 1965. They recommended
that only researchers be permitted to visit Surtsey. They
wanted to keep people away from the island as much as
possible in order to study it. They felt they had an opportunity to study how plant and animal life begins on
an island, and in what order life forms develop. Here
was a barren, sterile piece of land, much as the mainland
of Iceland undoubtedly was at one time. What would
happen next?

The first systematic study of life on Surtsey was begun
on May 14, 1964, by Sturla Fridriksson who is a biologist.
At that time he found only some micro-organisms, too
small to be seen with the eye alone. Both butterflies and
flies were observed during the summer, and numerous

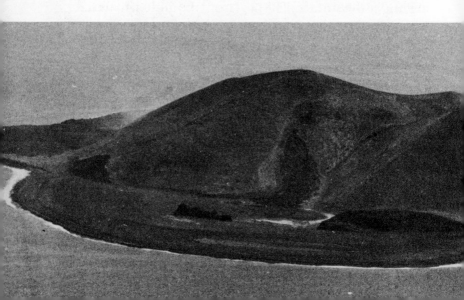

gulls and other birds visited the island that year, but none took up residence. The seeds of plants that grow along Iceland's coasts found their way to Surtsey—some by the water, some carried by the wind, and some on the feet and in the droppings of birds. Occasionally a live plant drifted ashore. But not until the summer of 1965 did the first plant sprout from seed, grow, and blossom. That plant was a sea rocket, a plant that grows on the southern shores of Iceland.

Several kinds of sea animals have washed ashore, including a baby harbor seal who was evidently lost from his mother.

And so Surtsey, which captured Olafur Vestmann's watchful eye that early morning in 1963 has managed to keep the attention of man for some time, first with its fire, then with its life.

Surtsey first appeared off the coast of Iceland in 1963. This new volcanic island gave scientists the opportunity to see how plant and animal life can begin on barren ground.

CHAPTER SIX

FIRE AND ICE

IT DOESN'T TAKE MUCH imagination to convince yourself you are on the moon while riding from Keflavik Airport to Reykjavik, Iceland's capital. Even though it's two o'clock in the morning, the summer sky is almost light, giving an eerie look to the lava-gnarled landscape. During the hour-long bus ride, you pass through mile after mile of flat land—a big pumice pancake—broken occasionally by an irregularly shaped boulder. The narrow ribbon of highway laid across this flat surface seems to be deserted except for the bus, which adds to your feeling of being a lunar explorer.

As you near the end of your ride, the countryside becomes hilly; you see some houses here and there and as you enter Reykjavik the ocean comes into view. But you find it difficult to shake off the feeling that you have just visited another planet.

Only a few people and cars are moving about the city at this time of day. It is so quiet and the place is so clean and neat-looking you feel you should wipe your feet and tiptoe in. The houses are made of cement or corrugated metal that has been painted a soft color and capped by brightly colored roofs. Lace curtains decorate each window.

As you get settled in your modern hotel room, you notice the radiator in the room is warm. Even summer nights can be chilly in Iceland. But from your window overlooking the city you notice the absence of smoke coming from the chimneys.

Then you remember reading that the entire city is heated by hot water that is pumped from natural underground pools. These pools lie close to pockets of *magma*, as underground molten rock is properly called. The temperature of the magma is probably around 2000° F, which means that the rocks surrounding the magma are also very hot, and some of this heat is transferred to the pools of water. By the time the water is pumped through insulated pipes into homes and other buildings, it is still over 200° F, almost boiling.

It is fortunate for the people in Iceland that they have these pools of magma to give off heat, as Iceland no longer has any forests and thus no wood to burn. There are no fields of coal nor any oil deposits to give them other fuels for heat.

But the magma does not always stay underground. On the average of every six or seven years, there is a major volcanic outburst. As magma from these pools comes to the surface, it loses most of the gas that had been dissolved in it. When it flows on the surface it is known as lava.

Iceland is well known for its fissure eruptions. This means the lava flows, not from a single vent, but from a crack in the earth's surface. Sometimes this crack is several miles long and from it pours forth an enormous amount of lava.

One of the most spectacular examples of such a flow took place in 1783 along the Laki fissure. The eruption began in early June and continued until the end of August. During that time lava completely filled a stream valley forty miles long and another valley that was fifty miles in length. The depth of lava averages one hundred feet, but in deeper gorges it will be from six hundred to seven hundred feet deep.

It began with a strange blue-colored fog hanging over the headwaters of the Skafta River. Then there were violent earthquakes in that area. For three days, ashes and steam soared into the sky in columns. The area was kept in semi-darkness by clouds. The lava began to pour from a fissure that was nearly fifteen miles long. Since the Skafta riverbed was lower than the rest of the countryside, the lava flowed into the riverbed and moved downstream, evaporating the river water. This water was turned into huge clouds of steam that ran just ahead of the red stream of molten rock. The river valley was two hundred feet wide and in places it was six hundred feet deep. But the lava soon filled it and crossed over a lowland area. In its path was a fairly large lake whose water was soon evaporated and replaced by lava.

By mid-June another fissure erupted close to the first one and followed the same path. This lava flow made its way over the partly hardened surface of the older lava. Since the depressions were mostly filled, it continued on past the former lake and followed a riverbed until it reached the waterfall, Stapafoss. Then, instead of water, fiery, molten rock plunged over the fall and made its way along the riverbed to the ocean.

On June 21, a fresh eruption produced more lava, and since the Skafta Valley was filled, the flow took another direction and filled another valley. Along with the destruction caused by the lava, there were heavy rains and floods. Twenty settlements were covered, either by lava or by water.

The ashes and vapors caused the most loss of life. People and animals became sick from the fumes and died. Poisonous ashes covered grazing land and killed crops. The ash contained such large amounts of fluorine, that when animals ate the ash-covered grass, the fluorine attacked their teeth and damaged their bones and joints. The poor animals could neither chew nor walk, and they starved to death.

About 10,000 people, almost one-fifth of the people who lived in Iceland, and nearly three-fourths of all their livestock, died. Fishing was very bad that year, and with most of their crops gone, the Icelanders were faced with starvation. Iceland counts this as her largest national disaster.

Iceland has actually been shaped by just such fissure eruptions. These outpourings of lava fill depressions that have been worn by rivers and glaciers. This explains the flatness of parts of the island. Similar fissure flows formed the Columbia Plateau in our states of Washington, Oregon, and Idaho.

Iceland's best known volcano is Hekla, which has erupted 16 times since the year 1104 A.D. It looks rather like an overturned boat, because its volcanic material comes out of a fissure about three miles long. Once when it erupted, beginning in 1766, the eruption continued for two years.

When Hekla first erupts, large amounts of dry materials that have accumulated—ash, dust and cinders—are shot out in clouds of steam. In 1947 when this occurred, wind blew the tephra a distance of 820 miles south where some of it fell on the decks of the *Sacramento*, less than 12 hours after the eruption began. The wind evidently shifted somewhat to the east, since 39 hours later volcanic dust fell in Helsinki, 1900 miles from Mount Hekla. Dr. S. Thorarinsson has calculated that during the first half hour of the 1947 eruption, tephra was ejected at the rate of 2.5 million cubic feet per second.

After the top layer of the fissure is cleared out, lava begins to flow from Hekla. The 1947 eruption continued for 13 months, and Dr. Thorarinsson estimated that during that time, 30 billion cubic feet of lava poured forth!

Farmers feared the ash-covered pastures would poison their animals, but heavy rains washed most of it away. Therefore, fewer animals died than in previous times. One hazard to animals was pockets of poisonous vapors that would collect in low places. Animals and birds would wander into the area and die from lack of oxygen. It was discovered that this gas was carbon dioxide, which was produced when some of the lava crystallized. Being heavier than air, the gas lay close to the ground, collecting in invisible pools where there were low places that were protected from the wind. This problem was solved by digging ditches away from these "pools." This allowed the gas to flow to more open, windy areas.

Another kind of volcanic eruption sometimes takes place in Iceland. This one occurs under the glaciers that cover about one-ninth of the country. The heat from these volcanic outbursts will melt the ice next to the ground, but not all the way to the surface of the glacier. This causes a lake to form *under* the glacier. Eventually the water will escape in a huge burst, causing a flood.

In 1934, people began to suspect that such a flood was about to take place when they noticed a slight increase in the amount of water in the Skeidara River. This river is one of the outlets for water that normally melts from a glacier named Vatnajökull. This glacier is three times the size of Rhode Island and covers the Grimsvötn Volcano. The increase in the flow of water was first noticed on March 22. By March 24, the river held three times its normal amount of water and it was still rising. Two days later the volume had increased to ten times its largest summer flow.

Usually the water came from a single ice cave at the edge of the glacier. Now it came from several places along the glacier's edge. As the amount of water gushing forth increased, new outlets formed. Finally, the force of the water knocked out the ice between openings, allowing the water to escape with a rush from an opening three miles wide. The pressure of the water forced huge chunks of ice to break away from the glacier and to be carried downstream.

This outpouring increased steadily until about noon on March 31. Then, dramatically, it got smaller and smaller so that by the next morning the river was back to its normal flow.

These floods are called *jökulhlaups*, which in Icelandic means "glacier bursts." They are not known to take place anywhere but Iceland, where one occurs about every ten years.

The Icelanders have not in the past known when to expect a jökulhlaup, but now they hope to have advance warning from weather satellites that go overhead. These weather stations can detect, through infrared measurements, "hot spots" under the surface of the earth. Scientists can't stop these floods but they can prevent people from being killed if they know when and where a flood might occur.

In reading about these things, we should remember that the underground chambers of magma give us more than destructive volcanoes and floods. Without the heat from these liquid rocks, people would find it very difficult to survive in Iceland. In addition to heat for their homes, Icelanders use the hot water from underground pools to warm greenhouses that supply them with fresh fruits and vegetables the year round.

In addition, this hot water gushes forth from geysers with great regularity, which entertains the many tourists who come to Iceland. And of course, the colorful mud pots that are formed when a geyser vent is covered by dirt and clay are interesting to watch. More practically, the energy gained from the hot water is needed to run the industry of the island.

All in all, Icelanders feel they gain more than they lose from living on an island that covers an unpredictable pot of molten rock.

CHAPTER SEVEN

THE VOLCANO THAT SPREAD CIVILIZATION

EMILY VERMEULE STOOD in the deep trench, looking at the decorated plastered walls the diggers had uncovered. Some of the walls had several layers of plaster—a black sponge print on a white background, covered by another layer with brown decorations on a cream background. Next to it was another done in pink and green. This type of decoration is called *fresco* (painting on wet plaster). These were done by the people who lived there 3500 years ago. Mrs. Vermeule had come to the island of Thera, off the coast of Greece, from the United States where she taught archeology and Greek. She felt a little depressed at the amount of work to be done and the fact that they would only be able to work a few weeks that summer. But her main feeling was one of excitement and this was due to the completeness of the houses they were uncovering.

The basements of the houses were full of unbroken storage pots that still contained grain and oil. There were weights from the weaving looms and by the hearth-side were cooking utensils. There were stone lamps with soot still on them. Mrs. Vermeule later wrote, ". . . the excavators felt vividly the presence of the . . . people whose lives had been changed so unexpectedly by powers inside the island under their feet."

The unexpected change that took place on Thera was caused by a volcano that erupted about 1403 B.C. At that time Thera, or Santorini as it is sometimes called, was inhabited by a group of people called Minoans. There were about one million Minoans living in a dozen cities on Crete and on other close-by islands, such as Thera. These people had a very advanced culture for that time. On the nearby mainland of Greece, the tribal people were still very primitive, living in crude huts. The Minoans, on the other hand, lived in modern houses and palaces decorated by lovely frescoes. They made beautiful vases, had a rather advanced sort of writing, and took part in various sports events. Their merchant fleets sailed to all the major ports of the Mediterranean Sea. There they sold their goods and brought home foreign products they needed.

Historians have known for a long time that about the fifteenth century B.C. the Minoan society suddenly all but vanished. The grand cities evidently were destroyed. Only on the western side of the island of Crete and occasionally on Greece's mainland were later traces of Minoans found. Approximately the same time, the Mycenaean civilization took an unexplained upward swing. It is approximately then that the written history of Greece begins.

For many years it was assumed that the Minoan society was destroyed by invaders, and that only a few escaped and carried their culture to Mycenae and the mainland. The refugees brought the Greeks their alphabet, their arts, and their games. They taught the primitive people there to work with bronze and gold, skills they had not had before.

It was not until the late 1800's that men accidently found houses buried under 100 to 150 feet of tephra. The men were miners, on Thera to dig the white ash which was used to make cement for the Suez Canal. Acres of it were carried away by ships that docked under the white cliffs. A French geologist, Ferdinand Fouqué, wrote a book that appeared in 1879 in which he described a pre-Greek six-room house that he had helped uncover. He gave a detailed record of the condition of the house and articles found in it. It seems only one person was killed at the time the house was covered with ash. That was an old man caught beneath a collapsed roof. How unlike Pompeii where bodies were found all around. Perhaps the Therans took to their boats before the destruction.

The French government sent two men out to investigate the ruins, but no follow-up expeditions occurred afterwards. Then in 1883 Krakatoa exploded and showed the world how powerful a volcano could be. For a brief time there was renewed interest in Thera, but it died out for lack of money for excavating. The world's attention was focused on other places and Thera was left to grape growers and miners.

It was because of the curiosity of Dr. Angelos Galanapoulos, a *seismologist* (a scientist who studies earthquakes) from the University of Athens, that the world again became interested in Thera. He went there in 1956 to investigate an earthquake. That was no great event, because this area had been having minor earthquakes and volcanic eruptions as long as people can remember. What interested him was a house at the bottom of a mine shaft—a house covered by 100 feet of volcanic ash. Dr. Galanapoulos found some bones which he asked scientists to "date" for him, along with a piece of wood he had taken from the house. By a special method, called *carbon-14 dating*, they estimated that the people had died and the tree had been cut around 1403 B.C. Dr. Galanapoulos remembered an article, written by Professor Spyridon Marinatos in 1939, which claimed the Minoan civilization was wiped out by a volcano, not destroyed by wars. Dr. Marinatos suggested that there had been a volcanic explosion on Thera that was even bigger than Krakatoa. Such an eruption on Thera could explain the sudden disappearance of the Minoans and the destruction of their cities. It could have been responsible for the large amounts of pumice on Crete's northern shore. Then World War II came along, and again the world turned its attention to other problems.

Dr. Galanapoulos had some other suggestions to add to those of Dr. Marinatos. He suggested that the legendary lost city of Atlantis might have been located on Thera.

For hundreds of years, scholars have argued about the lost land of Atlantis. Plato, a Greek philosopher who lived in the fifth century B.C., wrote a story about a man named Solon, who 200 years earlier had gone to Egypt. While Solon was in Egypt he was told by the priests that long ago "there dwelt in your land the fairest and noblest race of men which ever lived: of whom you and your whole race are but a seed or remnant. But there occurred violent earthquakes and floods, and in a single day and night of rain, all your warlike men in a body sank into the earth, and the island of Atlantis disappeared beneath the sea." Plato even described the size of the island as being 800,000 square miles. He said Atlantis was destroyed 9000 years before Solon's time.

Since Plato was so well respected, it was felt by many that his story was factual—but scientists through the years were unable to find a place where the sunken island might be. It was too large to fit in the Mediterranean. Others felt it was a kind of "science fiction" and not meant to be taken as truth. And so the argument has continued for many years.

Dr. Galanapoulos discovered that if all the figures in Plato's story were divided by ten, the sizes, distance, and dates would fit the Theran eruption. Perhaps Solon misread the Egyptian symbol for "100" as "1000."

Galanapoulos remembered a Greek legend about the greatest flood in history of Greece. A mythical character named Deucalion heard that Zeus, the chief god of the Mediterranean had become disgusted with the human race and decided to flood the earth and drown everyone. Deucalion found out about this and built a boat. When the floods came, he and his wife got in the boat and drifted for nine days until the floods went away. In Greek mythology, Deucalion was the nephew of Atlas, the first king of Atlantis. Did this flood have anything to do with the sinking of Atlantis?

Dr. Galanapoulos also remembered seeing a translation of an ancient Egyptian papyrus, written about the time of Thera's great eruption. These writings describe a time of prolonged darkness, flood, plague, and days when the sun was "in the sky like the moon."

"Confusion seized the eyes," the papyrus reads. "No one could leave the palace for nine days. Now these nine days were in violence and tempest; none . . . could see the face of his fellow."

Were these the same nine days that Deucalion and his wife spent adrift during the mythical flood?

"O that the earth would cease this noise," the papyrus continues. "The towns are destroyed . . . Upper Egypt has become wasted."

The papyrus complains that trade with Keftiu (the Egyptian word for Crete) had been cut off.

Dr. Galanapoulos kept these things in his mind until 1965 when he read a research paper that described some samples of sediment drilled deep out of the bottom of the Mediterranean Sea. These samples showed two widely separated layers of ash, such as is found on Thera. They calculated that the oldest layer was laid down about 23,000 B.C., and the one nearer the surface about the fifteenth century B.C. The layers were thicker around Thera and became progressively thinner the farther away from the city they got. The area of sea and land on which the ash fell could then be plotted on a map. The guess was made that the ash was carried more to the southwest because of the direction of the wind.

Further investigation showed that the present island of Thera is but a section of the rim of the old caldera. Under the surface of the water, the old crater is measured at four miles across—four times as large as the hole left in the submerged part of Krakatoa. From the size of the crater, the depth of the tephra, and the distance it was carried, scientists have speculated that the Thera explosion could have been nearly four times as great as Krakatoa.

Scientists think now that when the old Thera blew out its top, it left such a huge vacant space in the magma chambers underneath the mountain that what was left of the mountain collapsed into the hole. This left only a few islands jutting above sea level at the rim of the underwater caldera. What we now know as Thera is one of these rim islands. This dropping of the mountain's sides into the crater undoubtedly caused huge waves like the one formed when Krakatoa collapsed. The almost 100-foot-high waves must have hit the coast of Crete with a 200-mile-per-hour force and then continued on to the Upper Egyptian coast. It even left its mark on the ancient port of Ugarit in Syria, 640 miles away.

Dr. Galanapoulos feels the heavy fallout of volcanic ash that destroys crops and poisons fish may have produced the Ten Plagues that are told about in the Bible. He suggests the enslaved children of Israel may have made their famous flight to the Promised Land after this volcanic disaster hit Egypt.

Dr. Galanapoulos told an American naval engineer, James W. Mavor, Jr., of the Woods Hole Oceanographic Institution, what he knew and guessed from this knowledge. Mr. Mavor became so enthused that he went back to the United States and announced to the American press that he knew where the lost Atlantis was buried.

He persuaded Mrs. Vermeule to investigate the matter. She urged her friend Dr. Marinatos, who taught prehistoric archeology at the University of Athens, to supervise the project. Again the project nearly failed for lack of money to carry it out. During the summer of 1967, a number of scientists, most of whom paid their own way, were helped by forty miners, loaned to them by the owner of a local pumice mine. These people dug a series of trenches in the ash of Thera. They made drawings of their findings, and wrote descriptions of all that was seen and taken away. There was so much to do and so little time in which to do it. Everywhere people turned, something new and important came into sight. But they came away feeling that they had taken part in the beginning of a great adventure.

Dr. Marinatos felt that future excavations should be done by tunneling underground. He wanted an underground museum, with the city being dug out of its ash shroud, leaving the thick shell of pumice overhead and the vineyard still planted on the surface. In this way tons of ash would not have to be disposed of and the old civilization could be studied without destroying the new. Visitors could walk through the tunnels and see how people lived there more than 35 centuries ago.

Along with this dream of an unusual museum, Dr. Marinatos insisted that the excavating be done carefully and slowly. He even plans to keep a large section of it undug, so that in the next century scientists can use new techniques for solving the problems.

Scientists and scholars are still arguing about whether Atlantis is Thera or not. But one discovery that is certain is that Thera's explosion did move the Minoan culture from Crete to the Greek mainland. The Greeks improved it, passed it on to succeeding generations of Europeans who gave up their primitive ways and became more like the Greeks—or should we say more like the Minoans?

CHAPTER EIGHT

THE
BIRTH
OF A
FRIENDLY
VOLCANO

DIONISIO POLIDO WAS a Mexican Indian, a member of the Tarascan tribe. He lived in a tiny village called Parícutin. Before the mid-winter of 1943 there was nothing very special about Parícutin village or Senor Polido. But by the end of February of that year, in spite of a world war, everyone had heard of both the village and the simple farmer.

Parícutin was located almost 200 miles due west of Mexico City, high in the volcanic mountains of southern Mexico. It was perched on the edge of a shallow basin, which had been formed by many small, long-extinct volcanic cones. These low hills were covered with dense forests of pine and oak, not unlike the forests of the eastern United States. The Tarascan Indians had managed to clear some of these forests from the low lands for growing corn.

Dionisio Polido was a fortunate man, for he owned nine acres of cleared land near the center of the basin, only a mile or so from his home in the village. The soil was black from the crumbled lava of the numerous volcanoes that had lain quietly for many years.

Polido was also a good farmer. He planned his spring planting carefully and well in advance. No one was surprised when on the morning of February 20, he announced to his wife that today they would go to their field and prepare for its plowing.

Not very many farmers of Parícutin village were concerned about their fields that day, for earthquakes had shaken the area almost constantly during the past week. They had begun eight days ago, with a few, very mild shocks. Each day, the village was shaken four or five times and it seemed to the frightened Indians that each shock was a little stronger than the last. Just the day before, Parícutin was wracked by about 300 separate shocks, some of them strong enough to make cracks in the walls of their houses. In spite of all of this however, Polido was determined to visit his field.

The Indian farmer, his wife, and a neighbor who had offered to work in Polido's field, walked slowly over the small corn field. Polido's mind saw his land next summer, covered with green corn stalks. It was going to be a good year for growing corn, he thought to himself. The soil felt warm to his bare feet—perhaps too warm for early February.

At about four o'clock in the afternoon, the three Indians heard a low rumble and looked up from their work. "Is that thunder?" Polido's wife asked. They searched the sky but found it clear. Soon another rumbling noise reached them, and the ground shook slightly beneath their bare feet. "Another earthquake," Polido told them. "It will pass."

But the grumbling from the ground did not pass. Instead it continued to grow stronger and stronger. Then they saw the smoke. At first Polido thought the old corn stalks that lay in his field had caught fire, and he rushed toward the column of smoke. But he found no fire. Instead, he discovered the three-inch-wide spiral of black smoke came from a hole in the ground, and that here the sound of the growling earth was louder still.

Frightened, Polido ran back to the village of Parícutin, where he told his neighbors of the strange sight he had seen. None of the villagers could explain what was happening out there in Polido's corn field, so they became very frightened. A message was sent to the Presidente of San Juan, a larger city a few miles away. Soon a group of men arrived to look at the strange smoke. These men from San Juan reached the field at seven o'clock, only three hours after Polido first noticed the smoke. They found that in this short time the tiny hole in the earth had increased in size until it had become a huge pit, 30 feet across. From its mouth billowed a cloud of black ash containing glowing stones the villagers described as "sparks." Small stones were being thrown into the air to a height three times as tall as a man. A thick layer of dust had begun to cover Polido's field for several feet around the edge of the pit. The noise coming from the crack in the ground was terrifying to the

Indians and the smell of sulfur was so strong they were driven back from its edge.

Shortly after dark that evening explosions began shaking the houses of both Parícutin and San Juan so badly the villagers could not sleep. From Parícutin a bright red glow could be seen, coming from the direction of Polido's field. Bolts of lightning ripped through the dust cloud throughout the night.

Early the next morning the villagers again walked to the field. There, instead of the huge hole in the ground they had expected, they found a small mountain, about 40 feet high. At the top of the hill was an opening, and from this small crater came a steady stream of gases, ash, cinders, and larger rocks.

"It is a volcano!" one of them exclaimed. "A volcano is being born!"

Hurriedly, messages were sent to Mexico City and from there to the rest of the world. The next day, within 48 hours after it all began, scientists from both Mexico and the United States were camped beside the new volcano. For the first time in the history of man, scientists had the opportunity to watch the development of a volcano from its very beginning. As a result, more information about the development of volcanic mountains was gathered during the next nine years than had ever been known before. The new mountain was named Parícutin, in honor of Polido's village.

The first few months of Parícutin's life were noisy ones. The explosions increased in loudness and the time between them was only a matter of a second or two. Most of the material that came from the crater was solid. Clouds of ash and cinders rose to a height of 20,000 feet over the top of the mountain, and slowly settled to the ground. The tiny ash particles filled the air, and blotted out the sunlight, almost as if a storm were brewing. Slowly, the ash settled to the ground, smothering the plants, killing the trees, filling wells and choking streams. In the villages of Parícutin and San Juan, the roofs of houses became so heavily covered with the ash that many collapsed. Ash fell as far away as Mexico City—almost 200 miles.

In addition to the small-sized ash and cinders, the volcano occasionally threw out larger rocks, some the size of houses. The scientists discovered that these large rocks were of two different types. One, called a *bomb*, was actually melted lava that was thrown from the crater. As the bombs flew through the air, they cooled and often became solid before they hit the ground. Many were hard enough to crack when they struck, although some remained soft enough to splatter like a dropped pan-cake as they landed. The other type of large rock thrown by the volcano is called a *block*. Blocks were always solid and apparently were rocks that had been ripped off the side of the throat of the volcano by the passing lava. Some of these blocks were found a half a mile away from the cone.

The blocks and bombs that were thrown out by Parícutin took several seconds to fall back to the earth. Since the explosions followed each other by only a second or two, there were times when the air was filled with flying rocks, some weighing many tons. At night the glowing rocks looked like a huge fireworks display. Streaking chunks of fire arched high into the air every second or two.

Two views of the Mexican volcano, Parícutin, emphasize the drama of night and the reality of day.

Most of the solid material thrown out by Parícutin fell close to the volcano. In this way, the cone of the volcano was rapidly built up. The mountain grew 550 feet during its first week of life. After ten weeks it was more than 1000 feet tall, and by the end of its first year and a half, Parícutin became a full-sized mountain, standing over 1500 feet above the surrounding plain. A couple of years later it had grown to its full height of almost 2000 feet.

At first, very little lava flowed out of the volcano. On the second day, someone noticed a large crack was opening in the ground about 1000 feet north of the base of the cone and that lava had started to ooze out. This lava was very thick, like toothpaste. It was slowly squeezed out of the fissure and moved westward at about three feet per hour. When it stopped six weeks later, it had formed a broken, jagged mass of dark rock more than a mile long and a half mile wide.

Scientists think the solid material that was thrown from the mouth of the volcano was mostly rock that had blocked the pathway of the melted lava below the mountain. When it is extremely hot, magma contains large amounts of gases, such as steam, that are dissolved in the melted rock. As the magma cools and the rock begins to harden into crystals, the gases are released. Unless the steam can escape into the air, it will collect in large bubbles in the magma. As a result, more and more pressure builds up until the solid rocks above are blown out. This relieves the pressure a little and allows the lava to rise up the vent of the volcano.

Lava rarely flows over the top of a volcano's cone. As the lava rises higher up the vent, its weight pushes sideways with a greater and greater pressure. This pressure causes the earth's crust to be pushed outward, and large cracks often appear in the ground for some distance around the volcano cone. Usually the lava pours out through one or more of these cracks. Then, with the pressure released, the surface of the earth slumps back again, forming a depression.

Parícutin continued to "clear its throat" for four months, throwing out an almost constant stream of solid materials. The village of Parícutin had disappeared beneath a thick layer of soft ash, and the trees for miles in all directions were drooping, their leaves yellow and dying. All of the wildlife, even the birds, had abandoned the little valley, and nothing living dared approach the constantly exploding cone except the scientists who had built a small hut nearby.

In early June the scientists noticed that a number of large cracks had appeared in the sides of the cone, indicating the pressure under the earth was increasing. From an airplane, they were able to look directly down into the crater. It was nearly full of melted lava. Its top, cooled by the contact with the air, was almost solid and large blocks of rock floated in it like icebergs.

On June 15, 1943, the mountain was shaken by a violent explosion. A large fissure, 50 feet wide and 300 feet high, opened in the side of the cone itself and more pasty lava began to flow out. During the next few days seven more explosions were heard and seven more lava flows burst from the side of the cone.

Parícutin's new lava flow was thick and moved very slowly. Even while moving down the steep sides of the cone, its speed was rarely more than 100 feet per hour, although one flow did travel its first 1500 feet in about 15 minutes. Because of this slow movement, it was easy for the government of Mexico to move people out of its way. Therefore, even though both the village of Parí-cutin and the city of San Juan were destroyed by the volcano, not a single person was killed.

Since the lava was full of gas, bubbles formed once in a while, and then burst with a loud bang that sounded like a rifle. At times, these bursting bubbles splattered lava for more than 100 feet.

As the lava flowed down the hill, its surface cooled quickly when it touched the air. As it cooled, it became thicker and moved even more slowly. The hotter lava near the fissure soon began to pile up behind the rapidly cooling front, and the lava sheet became thicker and thicker. In some places over 30 feet of lava were deposited by a single flow.

The formation of a fissure in the side of the cone often caused the mountain above the fissure to collapse into the lava flow. Since the temperature of the lava was only barely above the melting point of rock, the rocks from the collapse were often carried along with the lava flow without being melted. Piles of this debris can still be seen, sticking up from the surface of the solid lava flow, many miles away from the volcano's cone.

In October, 1943, it appeared that another mountain was going to be born. A small crack appeared in the solid lava at the base of the now-tall mountain. Solid rocks began to be thrown out, and soon a little cone was built around the opening. The new cone grew to about 300 feet in height, and was named *Zapicho*, which means "little son" in Spanish. This smaller cone rapidly filled with lava, and a fissure appeared in its side. As the lava oozed through, the entire side of the cone collapsed, leaving a horseshoe-shaped mountain, similar to hundreds of others in Mexico.

The birth of this new volcano excited the scientists camped nearby, for many of them had not arrived on the scene until after Parícutin had grown into a fairly large mountain. But the "little son of Parícutin" was not to live long. Less than three years later a fissure opened in the side of the mountain above it and a huge lava flow buried the tiny hill.

As the year 1943 came to a close, Parícutin again changed its pattern. Far away from the main cone, dozens of fissures began to open up in the ground. From each of these came a flow of thick, doughy lava. Some of these streams flowed for five miles before cooling and stopping. The scientists who were studying the volcano at the time thought these new fissures were caused when the underground magma chambers collapsed. They think the chambers were left unsupported when the main magma mass moved toward the main vent.

Parícutin continued to throw out solid rocks and to spread large, slow-moving fields of lava over the area for almost nine years. Then, quite suddenly in 1952, the mountain became silent. But in those nine years the mountain, which had been so active, had grown to be almost 2000 feet high, and had covered an area of 100 square miles with ash, rocks, and lava. It has been estimated that over *seven million* pounds of this material was spread over the ground!

While Parícutin did some damage during its lifetime, it cost no human lives. In addition, it taught scientists a great deal about how volcanoes work. And, during its lifetime it was visited by thousands of tourists and sight-seers, who were given the thrill of their lives. It is little wonder that Parícutin has been given the nickname, "Mexico's Pet Volcano."

CHAPTER NINE

A
VOLCANIC
LABORATORY

THE WATER NEAR THE MIDDLE of the Pacific Ocean, near the Tropic of Cancer, is more than 15,000 feet deep. Across the bottom of this section of the ocean a large crack runs from northwest toward the southeast. Millions of years ago, lava began to flow from several points along this fissure, probably beginning first at the northwestern end. As was the case with Surtsey and other volcanic islands, the lava poured out onto the ocean bottom, slowly building a mound of solid lava. Finally, the first island in the area broke the surface of the water.

As thousands of years went by, the volcanic activity moved southeastward along the crack. More and more islands broke through the surface of the ocean and into the open air. Now a chain of 122 islands has formed, stretching over 1600 miles in the Pacific.

All of these volcanoes seem dead at the present time, except the ones that form the island of Hawaii farthest to the southeast.

The only large city on Hawaii is a busy port of nearly 30,000 people, named Hilo. Above Hilo towers the state's only active volcanoes—Mauna Loa and Kilauea. Down a shallow valley between these two peaks runs a little river. From it, the city of Hilo takes its fresh water supply. But water is not the only thing that can wash down the valley and into Hilo. Many times in the past, streams of glowing lava have also rushed down the valley, and into the outskirts of the town. Whenever this happens, there is the fear that the lava will not stop, but will rush through the city to the sea.

In December, 1933, it seemed as if Hilo's time had come. Lava had broken through the sides of the mountains above the city, and had begun to spread down the slopes. At first, it had been hoped that the thin, fluid lava would cool and become solid before it reached the city. But after the flows moved into the little river valley, and were joined by other rivers of moving lava, it became almost certain that Hilo was in danger.

As preparations were being made to take the people out of Hilo, the officials requested help from Dr. Thomas Jaggar. Dr. Jaggar was a geologist who was stationed on Hawaii for the purpose of studying the volcanoes. He suggested that since it seemed unlikely the lava would stop before reaching Hilo, perhaps they should try something new. His startling suggestion was that the U. S. Air Force *bomb* the lava!

Dr. Jaggar knew that one of the reasons the Hawaiian lava flowed for so many miles before it became solid was that its surface cooled and hardened very quickly. With a crust over it, the lava lost its heat slowly. It remained fluid for a long time. Therefore, Jaggar reasoned, a few well-placed bombs might break this thick crust and allow the lava inside to escape. If this could be done, cooling should take place more quickly.

The day after Christmas, Dr. Jaggar and the ten Air Force pilots selected for the mission, flew over the lava flow. They found that it was rushing toward Hilo at the speed of about 800 feet per hour. The scientist carefully selected what he thought would be the proper spots for the bombs to fall and showed them to the pilots. Then he returned to his laboratory to wait for morning.

At dawn the next day, ten American bombers left their field near Honolulu, each carrying 1200 pounds of TNT bombs. First they dropped bombs on the mouth of the flow high up on the slopes of the volcanoes. Then they bombed the front edge of the flow.

Anxiously, Dr. Jaggar and the citizens of Hilo watched for results of the experiment. You can imagine how relieved they were to discover that by four o'clock in the afternoon the flow had slowed to only 150 feet per hour. By sunset the following day the flow had stopped altogether.

Of course, no one can say for certain that the lava would not have stopped before it reached Hilo, as it had in the past. The important point of this story is that for perhaps the first time in the history of man, a scientific attempt had been made to control the flow of lava.

And to learn enough about volcanoes to someday control them is the story of the volcanoes of Hawaii.

Dr. Jaggar was, in 1933, the Director of the Hawaiian Volcano Observatory, which he started in 1912. His job, and the job of his staff, was to watch over and measure the activity of the volcanoes on the island. As a result of the work of these scientists, we probably know more about these two volcanoes than any others in the world.

The main buildings of the Volcano Observatory are perched on the edge of Kilauea Volcano's three-mile-wide caldera. From here, the scientists can look directly down the 500-foot-high, sheer cliffs at the flat floor of the caldera. Here lies a famous lake of boiling lava that is the main point of activity for the volcano. A short distance away stands a little cone that erupted in 1959, providing the scientists and dozens of visitors with a spectacular display.

Less than 30 miles west of the observatory buildings is the peak of Mauna Loa. Standing nearly 14,000 feet above the sea, and nearly 30,000 feet above the ocean floor, Mauna Loa, and the island of Hawaii that it helped create, must be ranked as one of the world's largest mountains.

Hawaii was selected as the best location for the Volcano Observatory primarily because the volcanoes there are in almost constant eruption. Mauna Loa produces a major lava flow on the average of one every two years, and several more-or-less permanent lava lakes exist there. Another reason for the careful study of the Hawaiian volcanoes is that this is one of the few places where scientists can safely get very, very close to the point

*Boiling lava
from the Halemaumau volcano
in Hawaii
illuminates the night sky.*

*The frequent lava flows
of Mauna Loa
give the scientists at
the Hawaiian Volcano Observatory
the opportunity to study
volcanic eruptions
both before and
during the event.*

of eruption. Here it is possible to move both people and instruments right up to the shores of the glowing lava lakes, usually within minutes after they form. The scientists can collect ash and cinders as they fall to the ground, without much danger that a large block of rock will be dropped on them. It is possible for measuring instruments to be placed right into the erupting volcano's throat, without danger of an explosion catching the scientist in the open.

The purpose of this volcanic laboratory is to allow the scientists to study the ways in which volcanoes erupt. By this study they hope to be able to understand what happens under the ground before a volcano explodes. Even if scientists cannot discover how to control volcanoes, it seems likely that they will be able to predict *when* an eruption is about to take place. When they can do this, the loss of life from volcanoes will be much less.

The Hawaiian studies have already begun to show some evidence of success. In 1965, for example, they were able to predict new activity from a cone in the Kilauea caldera a *full two months* before it became active. And, what is perhaps more important, they knew two hours ahead, and could pinpoint almost exactly when the eruption would begin!

The first indications the scientists have that one of the volcanoes around them is about to become active is a change in the size of the cone. As the pressure builds up inside the magma below the volcano, the sides of the cone swell outward slightly, and become a little steeper. You may not be able to see this slight change in the slope on the outside of the cone of the volcano. But it can be measured by instruments, called tiltmeters. These instruments are so sensitive that they can detect a movement of $4/100$ of an inch in the rock!

In addition, the size of the fissures around the cone often increase as the magma pushes harder from below. The width of these fissures is measured daily. Sometimes the scientists can predict an eruption from this information.

A third measurement that is taken is of the earthquakes that sometimes go along with volcanic eruptions. As you have seen from the stories you have read in this book, the explosion of a volcano almost always produces earthquakes over a large area. What the scientists at the Hawaii Observatory are trying to find out is whether or not earthquakes always occur before an eruption and, if so, how they can be used to predict what will happen.

One instrument used to measure earthquakes is called a *seismograph*. This instrument is sometimes made of a heavy framework that is attached firmly to the rocks of the earth. From this framework hangs a heavy, free-swinging *pendulum*. A mirror in the pendulum reflects a beam of light onto a roll of photographic film that slowly passes by the machine. When the earth trembles, the framework also moves, since it is attached to the rocks. But the pendulum is so heavy that it remains still. The result is a wavy line, made by a beam of light shining on the trembling piece of film.

During a normal day, even when none of the volcanoes on Hawaii are erupting, the observatory's seismographs pick up the shock waves of as many as 1000 earthquakes, most of which are too slight to be felt by human beings. But they show movement somewhere, far beneath the earth's surface. By finding the location of the worst shocks, scientists can often predict where lava will come to the surface.

An important discovery made by the scientists on Hawaii who use the seismographs is that the earthquakes that occur just before an eruption are of a special kind. They have found that the earth's surface moves up and down with a regular rhythm, about twice each second. This movement is too slight to be felt by human beings, but the seismographs show it easily. Apparently, these slight, very regular shocks are caused by the flow of magma below the surface. From these shocks, scientists can predict when lava will erupt onto the surface of the earth, usually within a matter of a few hours.

Perhaps the most interesting feature of the eruptions of Mauna Loa are the lava "curtains" and "fountains" that usually occur. After the walls of the mountain are pushed outward, large cracks appear in the floor of the caldera. Lava, which is very fluid, then fills the fissures, and the steam trapped below forces some of the melted rock to spray high into the air along the crack. The result is a "curtain of fire," sometimes reaching a height of 500 feet.

As the surface of the lava cools, the "curtains" become more and more narrow. Finally, the lava is sprayed from a fairly small opening, rather than from a large crack. The result is a towering "fountain" of glowing lava. Since the pressure of the steam is concentrated at only one spot, the fountains are often quite high. In 1959, one fountain was formed that shot lava upward for 2000 feet!

It is true that the information the scientists gather on Hawaii cannot, perhaps, be used to predict the behavior of all the volcanoes in the world. But it is likely that other scientists can learn something from the methods used on Hawaii and in this way study other volcanoes. When this is done, it may be possible for us to visit any volcano in the world we may wish to see in safety, just as we can now visit those of Hawaii.

CHAPTER TEN

THE VALLEY OF TEN THOUSAND SMOKES

CAPTAIN K. W. PERRY, skipper of the U.S. steamer *Manning*, stood on his deck watching the dock crews load coal aboard. The time was four o'clock in the afternoon of June 6, 1912. The port was St. Paul, a small village on the Alaskan island of Kodiak. Glancing idly across the island toward the west he noticed a peculiar cloud that seemed to be rapidly growing from the horizon. "A snow cloud," he thought. "Late in the year for snow, I should think." Making a mental note to watch the progress of the storm, he wrote the time in his log.

An hour later the cloud covered about one-fourth of the western sky and a light snow began to fall. Captain

Perry stepped back onto the deck, so as to see the cloud better. Suddenly, he realized that it was not snow that was drifting ahead of the gray mass above him, but tiny, floating bits of ash!

By six o'clock the face of the cloud had passed over the ship and the fall of ash had increased. Perry called to his ship's officers, ordering them to get the entire crew on deck and to begin cleaning the fine layer of dust from the ship. "We have only three hours until sunset," he told them. "I want the ship clean by then."

But Captain Perry was wrong about the amount of time his crew had to clean the ship. Within an hour— a full two hours before sunset, darkness fell. "A black night," Perry described that afternoon in his log. Throughout the long night ash continued to fall, while lightning flashed and thunder rolled through the blackness. At nine the next morning, a dim sun shone weakly through the reddish haze. Five inches of ash covered everything in sight—houses, wharves, ships. Streams and wells were choked with the white, snow-like stuff, and the *Manning* began to supply fresh water to the citizens of St. Paul.

By noon the *Manning's* crew had no sooner finished clearing the ship of the heavy ash than it began again. This time the darkness came even earlier, around two in the afternoon. The smell of sulfur choked the sailors as they used their brooms, shovels, and fire hoses to clear the decks, this time by lantern light. The sound of avalanches of ash could be heard dully as the accumulated weight on the sides of the hills became too great and tons of debris poured down the slopes. Strange-shaped lightning flashes cut through the darkness and the men talked of the stories they had heard of Pompeii.

By the afternoon of June 8, the fall of ash slowed somewhat and the people of St. Paul could dimly see again. Occasionally, the ground would shake beneath their feet, and their lungs choked with dust and ash, but it was apparent the worst was over.

It was clear to every educated person in the area that a volcano had erupted with a tremendous explosion. On June 6, its sound was heard in the city of Juneau, almost 750 miles due east, and its dust had settled to the earth 900 miles away, in Ketchikan. Near Iliamma Bay, over 100 miles away, it was reported later "the earth never ceased to move for twelve hours." But no one knew where the active volcano was.

Several days later, when the mail steamer *Dora* arrived at Seward, the first real information was flashed to the world. On the sixth, the *Dora* had been cruising in the Shelikof Straits that separate Kodiak Island from the Alaskan Peninsula. At about three in the afternoon, the *Dora's* crew heard a tremendous explosion and saw a heavy column of what appeared to be smoke rise over the mainland. The skipper of the steamer took a bearing on the smoke and decided that it came from the 7500-foot-tall Mount Katmai that stood some 55 miles away.

By six that evening, the *Dora* was groping her way through a heavy, unnatural blackness. "We could not even see the water passing the side of the ship!" the captain reported later.

At first, it seemed the little ship might make the safety of one of the many harbors of Kodiak Island, but darkness closed in on them before they could find a safe channel. Setting a course for the safer open sea, the *Dora* felt its way up the coast through the darkness, which lasted for 24 hours. "Even the birds couldn't fly through the clouds," the crew reported later. "Dozens of them fell to the deck all through that long night."

Geologists in the United States were surprised at the *Dora's* report that Mount Katmai had erupted. The ancient mountain was a volcano, all right. There was no doubt of that. But it had lain quietly for so many generations that even the local Indians had no legends about it. Any one of a hundred other Alaskan volcanoes might be expected to erupt at any time, since dozens of them constantly produced steam. Minor, local earthquakes were an everyday occurrence in the huge territory. But it was difficult to believe that the *Dora's* captain had not made a mistake in his sightings. However, after a search of several weeks, some eye-witnesses were found, and their stories seemed to show that the report from the *Dora* was correct.

Near the coast, almost 20 miles south of Mount Katmai, was the little Indian village of Katmai. During the summer, the village's entire population moved farther down the coast to the fishing village of Cold Bay, where they could find work. In the year 1912, this movement of the village people had taken place on June 4, just two days before the explosion. For some unexplained reason, two families had stayed behind this year, and thus became the nearest human beings to survive the eruptions.

It was not until after the explosions began and the air was filled with flying ash and rocks that these families finally fled their village. In their tiny skin boats, they paddled furiously south along the coast and away from the thundering giant behind them. They arrived safely at Cold Bay, their boats badly damaged by flying pebbles, and gasped out their story to their friends. "The top of Katmai hill burn off!" they said.

It wasn't until six years later that another eyewitness was found. An old man called "American Pete" was dying of tuberculosis when he was found by the leader of an American scientific party. Yes, he had been near the mountain that day, nearly as close as the Katmai villagers but on the other side, toward the north.

American Pete was the chief of a tribe of Indians who lived in a village called Savonoski, on the shores of Lake Naknek. The Savonoski Indians took fish from the lake and its streams. They hunted caribou, moose, and bear in a heavily wooded valley that ran toward the north from the base of Mount Katmai. At the opposite end of the valley from the mountain, they had built a cluster of huts to stay in overnight when they were hunting in the valley. American Pete had gone alone to the hunting camp on the afternoon of June 6.

"The Katmai Mountain blow up with lots of fire, and fire come down trail from Katmai with lots of smoke," he told the American scientist. "Me go fast Savonoski. Everybody get in skin boats. Dark. No could see. Hot ash fall."

No one will ever know whether there were other witnesses to the explosions of June 6, 1912, and it is likely that if there were, they did not survive. It is fortunate for American Pete that he "go fast Savonoski," for the valley that he was in changed suddenly that day, and every living thing in it died.

The rest of the world knew nothing about the changes in American Pete's valley until almost four years after the eruptions. And when the changes were reported, many people simply couldn't believe them!

The discovery of what happened in the valley was made by a team of scientists sent by the National Geographic Society in 1916. They were to climb and survey what was left of Mount Katmai. They found the top of the mountain had, indeed, disappeared—almost 1000 feet of it. In its place was a huge caldera that measured $3\frac{1}{2}$ by $2\frac{1}{2}$ miles, and almost a half mile deep. In the bottom of the caldera was a sparkling blue lake, with a tiny island that had been pushed up in its center. It was when the scientists began their survey of the northern slopes of the mountain that they first saw what was left of American Pete's valley.

Here was a long, narrow valley, not gently rolling and tree covered as they had expected, but almost perfectly flat. The director of the team described what he first saw like this: "Great columns of white vapor poured out of the fissured ground, rising gracefully until they mingled in a common cloud which hung between the walls of the valley. The whole valley as far as the eye could reach, was full of hundreds, no thousands—literally tens of thousands of smokes curling up from its floor." And, in this way, the "Valley of Ten Thousand Smokes" was discovered and named.

(Pages 118–119)
*The smoking volcano
is Mt. Katmai in Alaska.
To the right is the flat
expanse of land known as
the "Valley of the 10,000 Smokes."*

Another discovery was made by this group of scientists. To the west of Mount Katmai about five miles, they discovered a new, active volcano, which they named "Novarupta." This discovery may be even more important to the solution of the mystery of what happened in June of 1912 than the discovery of the Valley of Ten Thousand Smokes.

It was not until two summers later that a group of scientists could explore the valley carefully. Their most surprising discovery was that the flat floor of the valley was not caused by an ordinary flow of lava, as they had expected. Instead, they found the valley to be covered with a fine-grained sand that had apparently washed through the valley at the time of the eruptions.

It is now thought, by some scientists at least, that this sand was very, very hot at the time it flowed from the mountain. Probably, since it acted very much like a flowing liquid, it was mixed with a great amount of gas from the magma below the surface. As the super-hot gas rushed up through cracks in the earth, it must have picked up rocks and broken them into sand-sized particles. When this mixture of sand and gas reached the surface of the earth, it flowed down the valley, like Pelée's "glowing cloud." The major difference between this "cloud" and that of Mount Pelée would seem to be that the one that flowed through the Valley of Ten Thousand Smokes was very much heavier. Therefore, it hugged the ground, killing only those living things it actually touched.

And kill it did, but apparently no human beings were trapped by this "glowing cloud." When the scientists arrived in the valley they found the hot sand had burned all of the life from an area of 53 square miles. It buried the valley for a length of over 20 miles, and a width of about 9 miles at the widest point. At first, no one could guess how deep the sand lay in the valley. More recent studies show that, in places, the sand is 700 feet deep! The total weight of sand that flowed out into the valley must have been nearly 30 million tons!

After the sand had cooled and the gas had escaped, the floor of the valley began to explode. Evidence of this is seen in the hundreds of small volcanic craters that pock-mark the otherwise smooth sand. And then, through these craters or through fissures opened by the pressure below, steam began to escape. The scientists measured the temperature of the escaping gas. In many of the vents it was well over 500° F, and one had a temperature of nearly 1200° F. To give you some idea of how hot this hotter temperature is, it is nearly the melting point of aluminum, and well above the melting points of both lead and zinc!

The destruction of living things was so complete in the valley that the team of scientists found it necessary to bring in everything they would need in packs on their backs. This included not only their food, clothing and tents, but also all the wood they would need. Naturally, they did not want to pack in wood for their cooking fires, if they could help it. They soon discovered they could swing a cooking pot from a rope and lower it into one of the steam vents. After cooking a few meals this way, however, they found that the steam contained some type of acid. This acid ate into the ropes so that they were weakened and broke easily. Eventually, the acid steam even ate holes in the bottom of the iron pots!

Since 1916, many groups of scientists have studied the area around the Valley of Ten Thousand Smokes. This is now called Katmai National Monument, named for the large volcano in its center. As a result of all this study, there has been a new theory suggested, that perhaps explains what happened in 1912 a little more completely than did the stories of the Indian eye-witnesses. This new idea suggests that Mount Katmai was *not* the mountain that exploded. Instead, many scientists now think it was the new volcano, Novarupta, that erupted and threw so much ash and rock over the Alaskan Peninsula and Kodiak Island. It seems almost certain that it was Novarupta, or at least the magma below it, that produced the heavy "glowing cloud" that covered the valley.

But, if this idea is true, what happened to the top of Mount Katmai?

As you have seen in the previous chapters of this book, large calderas are generally formed by the *collapse* of the top of a mountain, rather than by its being blown completely away. Even the disappearance of the island of Krakatoa is explained primarily by supposing that most of the mountain fell into itself.

This newest theory on the collapse of Mount Katmai suggests that the vent of Novarupta opened into the same magma pocket that lies under Mount Katmai (and under the Valley of Ten Thousand Smokes). When Novarupta exploded so violently, the pressure on the magma must have been released. This must have allowed the whole magma to shift somewhat, leaving a hollow space below Mount Katmai, five miles away. Thus, the whole top of the mountain simply fell into the empty space left by the moving magma.

Will the thousands of steaming vents release enough of the pressure on the magma below Novarupta and the valley to keep it from erupting again? Scientists think this is probably what is happening since many of the vents have slowed or stopped their release of steam. But the chain of islands and the Alaskan Peninsula contain about 80 volcanoes, more than half of which are considered to be active. It seems probable that we will hear more about the volcanoes in this area in the future.

CHAPTER ELEVEN

OTHER AMERICAN VOLCANOES

LASSEN PEAK

IN NORTHERN CALIFORNIA, at the southern end of the Cascade Mountain Range, stands a 10,500-foot-tall mountain named Lassen Peak. Now the peak is surrounded by a National Park, but in 1914 the park had not been established. Only wilderness and a few settlers surrounded the "dead" volcano. But, on May 30, just eight years after an earthquake and fire destroyed San Francisco, Lassen came back to life with a fury that rivaled that of Mount Pelée.

The beginning of the first eruption of Lassen Peak within historical time was an unexciting one. Several people were near the mountain in late May, 1914. Harry Kaul was one of these. Kaul had evidence that the sleeping volcano was going to come to life a little before it actually did, but he did not realize what this evidence meant. On Thursday, two days before the eruption, he thought he heard thunder. But, when he left his cabin and looked into the sky, he saw that it was a perfectly clear night.

By the next afternoon, however, Kaul knew what had caused the thunder. At 2:30 on Friday, he felt an earthquake shock that was strong enough to shake the roof from his barn. This shock was felt in Susanville, which is over 50 miles away from Lassen Peak.

On the same day—Friday—a stage coach driver reported that he had seen "a white cloud" coming from the top of the mountain. That afternoon, Kaul and a group of his friends visited the top of the peak. Once there, they found that a small crater had formed, and that a small amount of cinders and pebbles had been thrown about. Not very excited, the settlers returned to their farms.

However, early in the morning on the first of June, the mountain broke out again, this time throwing out a few large blocks, some weighing as much as a ton. The crater at the top of the peak increased in size until it formed a huge crack, 60 feet wide and 250 feet long. The heat from the bottom of this hole was so great that snow covering the mountain's top melted and ran down into the fissure. When it reached the molten rock below, it immediately turned to steam and rose from the mountain top in large, white billows.

The activity continued, off and on, during the next year. The winter of 1914–15 was a particularly wet one in northern California. Huge amounts of melted snow flowed into the ever-widening crater, and were then poured back into the sky as steam. Some scientists have suggested that it was the cooling by this melted snow that brought on the violent eruptions experienced the next spring.

Whatever the cause, the character of the Lassen volcano changed that spring. During May of 1915, a mass of thick, slow-moving lava appeared in a crack that split the western side of the cone. The appearance of lava for the first time caused some concern among the neighbors on the mountain, and a careful watch was kept on

the west side of the volcano. The very next night a violent mudflow formed on the unwatched east side of the cone. It rushed down the slope and into the valleys of Hat Creek and Lost Creek, carrying 20-ton boulders along like they were grains of sand. This mudflow killed no one, and in the long run probably saved many lives, for it forced many of the settlers who lived nearest to the volcano to move to points farther away.

On May 22, 1915, the temperament of the volcano changed again, and again the change was for the worse.

Lassen Peak, in California, is sometimes referred to as "America's sleeping volcano." Its last period of activity occurred only a little over a half a century ago.

The thick lava had apparently clogged the vent, trapping the gases below ground, in the same way as did the lava of Mount Pelée. For three days the pressure grew and grew before it finally gained enough strength to burst through the side of the peak, near the top on the east side. A glowing cloud, much like the one that had destroyed Saint Pierre, rushed down the side of the mountain and into the creek valleys below.

Fortunately, no human beings were trapped by the hot gas, and it did little damage directly. However, its heat did melt large amounts of snow. This boiling water combined with mud and rocks, rushed through many tiny farms, crushing and burying everything in its path. Warned by the explosions and the mudflow of the previous days, the settlers and their families managed to move out ahead of the flow, and again no lives were lost.

As with Mount Pelée, Lassen built a final monument to itself as it died. After a couple of years of more mild eruptions, the grumblings within the earth became quiet. And then, silently, a solid tower of lava slowly rose from the crater. Then Lassen Volcano, the only volcano to have been active in the continental United States during historical times, went back to sleep. For years scientists could not be certain that it was not dead; however recent infrared measurements taken from orbiting satellites show it to be "hot."

Written records have not been kept in the United States except for the past few generations, so it is not known just how many volcanoes have erupted. Indians from all parts of the country have legends of mountains that breathed fire and smoke, but it is difficult to trace these rumors to their source. There is evidence of volcanic action in many parts of the United States other than Alaska and Hawaii, and scientists have been able to piece together some idea of what happened in some of these instances.

THE CASCADE RANGE

Lassen Peak marks the southern end of the whole range of volcanic mountains, which extends from northern California northward through Oregon and Washington and into Canada. You may have heard of some of the volcanoes in the Cascade Mountain Range. The highest is Mount Rainier, in Washington state. It is almost 14,500

Glaciers dot the sides of Washington State's Mt. Rainier. Standing almost 14,500 feet high, this volcano is the tallest in the Cascade Mountain Range.

feet high and, even though occasionally plumes of white steam drift from its crater, the mountain's sides are covered with more than two dozen glaciers. Mount Shasta is another well-known volcano of the Cascade Range. It lies in northern California, and is a neighbor of Lassen Peak. Shasta is over 14,000 feet high, but seems much taller since it towers more than two miles above the lower mountains that surround it. Mount Baker stands near the Canadian border and is more than 10,000 feet high, Mount Hood, a 12,000-foot peak near Portland, Oregon, and Mount Adams, a few miles to the

The snow-covered peak of Mt. Shasta lies in northern California. Its highest point above sea level is over 14,000 feet.

north, are all volcanic mountains that scientists think have become extinct only recently. All are rumored to have been active around 1840, but no one is absolutely certain of this.

The Cascade Range is a young set of mountains, according to the time scale used by geologists. About 60 million years ago the surface of the earth at the bottom of a shallow ocean began to buckle and wrinkle, due to tremendous forces from deep within the earth. Slowly, over hundreds of thousands of years, the land was lifted upward, out of the ocean water, until a new range of mountains was formed.

As often has happened in the past, the uplift of such a large block of land caused the rocks to break. Through these breaks, pockets of magma rose, and along the face of the Cascade Range active volcanoes began to form. One of the last of these was Mount Mazama, located in what is now southern Oregon.

MOUNT MAZAMA AND CRATER LAKE

The history of Mount Mazama must have been similar to that of many other volcanoes. Its sides show layers of ash and cinders lying between layers of what must have been rather thick, slow-moving lava. Apparently the volcano then became quiet and remained so for many, many years. As glaciers from the north carved into its sides and trees took root in the broken lava slopes, the plug in the volcano's neck became solid.

About 6500 years ago, Mazama came to life again. No one knows, of course, exactly what happened. Scientists are certain that at least one glowing cloud rushed down the side of the mountain, because the remains of burned and charred trees are found in the bottom of river valleys for distances of 30 miles around the mountain. These look very similar to the wooden articles found in Saint Pierre after Mount Pelée exploded on the island of Martinique.

Scientists cannot be certain how long this new series of eruptions lasted, but how they ended is quite apparent. The top half of the mountain simply disappeared! A small amount of this solid material was thrown into the air, falling in all directions around the volcano. The larger part of it, however, seemed to have fallen into the center of the mountain itself.

Crater Lake in southern Oregon is 2000 feet deep. Years ago a tiny volcano developed inside the old caldera and remains today as an island.

The result of this tremendous explosion was the formation of a large caldera, almost round and about six miles across. Slowly over the centuries since, the caldera has filled with water; today it forms a lake almost 2000 feet deep. This is the famous Crater Lake.

But the story of Mount Mazama and of the beautiful Crater Lake was not finished. Many years after the formation of the huge caldera, lava again began to flow from a crack in the bottom of the lake. As so often happens in large calderas, a smaller volcano developed, forming a small island in the middle of the sparkling blue lake.

THE COLUMBIA PLATEAU

Look at a map of the northwestern United States that shows where the mountains lie, and you will find a large, flat area in southeastern Washington and parts of adjoining Oregon and Idaho. This is the Columbia Plateau. It is the largest lava flow in the world, and covers an area of about 225,000 square miles.

The Columbia Plateau was formed between 25 million and 15 million years ago. By that time, the rugged mountains of our west coast had already formed. Then, apparently in the same way as it did in Iceland, the earth cracked in many places. Thousands of fissures, some of them probably several miles long, opened up. Tons of fluid lava poured out, flowed into the valleys, and began to slowly bury the countryside.

Geologists are certain that there were many, many different flows, since they can find layer upon layer of lava separated by the remains of lake animals and plants, trees, and even an occasional fossil of a large land animal. Therefore, they assume there were long periods of time between the eruptions—long enough for lakes to form, forests to grow on the broken-up lava, and animals to wander in from the outside. Then the lava flowed out again, burying everything under many feet of melted rock.

Eruptions of this quiet type continued for millions of years, until at last the high mountains themselves were completely buried. In some places the lava now lies almost a full mile deep!

CRATERS OF THE MOON

Near the eastern edge of the Columbia Plateau lies the National Monument called The Craters of the Moon.

And when you walk through this area of the United States, you might believe you are walking on the surface of the moon. Here you see small, perfectly shaped volcanic cones. Lava lies everywhere, frozen into fantastic shapes—even "waterfalls" of solid stone.

Lavas of both the very fluid type and the almost-solid type apparently flowed here at one time or another. The first has formed ropy or very smooth areas, while the less fluid lava broke into huge blocks that are scattered over large areas. Some of the lava became solid on its surface so rapidly that the underlying, more fluid lava flowed out, leaving several large caves or tunnels. Some of these even contain hanging columns like the stalactites in limestone caves of Carlsbad and Mammoth!

PETRIFIED TREES

At one time, about 50 million years ago, the border between what are now the states of Wyoming and Montana was covered with dense forests. Both evergreen and hardwood trees grew there, similar to those that now grow along the Gulf Coasts. Then, somewhere far to the east of what is now Yellowstone Park, one or more volcanoes erupted. They spewed tons of ash into the air, and these tiny particles were carried by the wind until they fell into the forests. Slowly the ash accumulated, much as it did in Pompeii, until the trees were covered by many feet of debris. The fall was always gentle, for few of the trees fell to the ground. Instead, they were buried standing as they grew.

Slowly, over many centuries the woody material of these buried trees was replaced by minerals carried into the now-solid ash by water. Eventually, each of the trees became replaced by stone.

*Sometimes the outer, softer layers
of a dead volcano will be worn and washed away,
leaving only the core of hardened lava,
such as the Devils Tower in Wyoming.*

Over the next 20,000 years, this story was repeated again and again! As soon as the ash cooled, seeds of new trees found support, and new forests grew above the old. After several hundred years, new eruptions occurred and a new layer of ash covered the new forests. In all, a total of 27 *layers* of petrified forests have been found in this area!

SCATTERED SKELETONS OF DEAD VOLCANOES

After a volcano dies, it is immediately attacked by both wind and water. Even hard, glass-like lava will be slowly broken up and carried away. The sides of the volcano mountain itself will sometimes be washed or blown away, leaving only the harder parts behind.

Since the vent inside the volcano is usually filled with lava, and the mountain itself is made of cinders and ash, we might expect that the softer materials of the outside would be washed away easily. When this happens, the lava in the vent is left standing like some strange monument. Shiprock in New Mexico is such a tower; Devils Tower of Wyoming is probably another.

Sometimes an underground crack in the earth will fill with lava. After the lava hardens, a sheet of rock is formed. When the water and wind uncovers these sheets, we call them *dikes*. Many dikes surround the Spanish Peaks of Colorado. One dike in South Africa is 300 miles long and four miles wide!

CHAPTER TWELVE

GEYSERS, HOT SPRINGS, AND PAINT POTS

"WHAT A STRANGE PLACE," you think as you stand looking at the quiet pool of water in front of you. If you hadn't ridden here in an automobile, through ordinary-looking country, you might believe that you were on some far-away planet. Surrounding you are dozens of pools of water, each with little clouds of steam rising from them. Nothing grows near the pools, and the rocks are not sharp and broken looking. Instead, each seems covered with what looks like petrified snow or ice.

Suddenly you hear a low rumbling noise that seems to come from beneath your feet. This is followed by a gurgling sound from the pool in front of you. As the

*The rims of some hot springs in
the Yellowstone National Park
are deposits of calcium carbonate
brought to the surface by boiling water
inside the springs.*

gurgling becomes louder you step back, not certain what is going to happen next. And it is a good thing you did!

The water in the pool is no longer quiet. Currents and tiny whirlpools appear, and the surface begins to roll, like a pot of water just coming to a boil. Then, a huge bubble of steam reaches the surface, and steaming water splashes over the rim of the pool.

The bubbles continue to rise for several minutes and each one seems to be a little larger than the one before. Without further warning the entire pool of water seems to leap into the air and fall, splashing and steaming, over the rocks around it. This is followed by a second eruption of water, higher than the previous one, and then a third and a fourth.

For many minutes the fountain of water continues to spew from the ground, at times reaching a height of over 100 feet.

The noise of the rushing water fills your ears, the heat of the falling water brushes your face, and you move further back to avoid the nearly boiling water that is hanging in a tall cloud before you.

And then, even more suddenly than it began, it is over. You have just witnessed one of nature's strangest sights, the eruption of a geyser.

GEYSERS

Where would you have to be to see this amazing sight? Geysers are fairly rare, but you might see them in Yellowstone Park. Or you might see them in Iceland, or in New Zealand. A few are to be found in Mexico, South America, and Japan. Indeed, you might find a geyser wherever there is, or recently has been, volcanic activity.

No one knows what causes geysers to erupt, especially those that put on their spectacular displays with almost clock-like regularity. At one time people thought the geyser pool was simply a very, very deep pit, and that the water at the bottom of the pit was being heated by the natural heat of the interior of the earth. But scientists now realize that the pressure far below the surface of the earth squeezes the rocks so tightly together that water cannot find its way through them. Apparently the heat that causes a geyser to explode is the same as the heat source of a volcano—a mass of magma not too far below the surface. Magmas lying near the surface of the earth do not always result in volcanoes that explode or pour out lava. Instead they sometimes produce a variety of unusual sights.

Unlike the magma below a volcano, magma that does not find a surface opening will not cool quickly. We can suppose that there are many such large masses of melted rock that have remained hot for thousands of years.

Geologists now think that below the geyser pool is a deep, probably narrow pit, most likely with many twists, turns, and side passages. Water, seeping through the rocks around the pit, flows into it and fills it to the top. As the water gets hotter from the magma below it, it cannot circulate easily, because of the crooked shape of the passageway. And the water deep below the surface becomes much hotter than the upper water.

The temperature at which water will boil depends upon the pressure on it. Perhaps you know that at sea level water will normally boil at about 212° F, but that high on a mountain it will boil at a much lower temperature. This is because the air pressure at the higher altitude is less than it is at sea level. However, if the pressure is increased, the temperature at which water boils is raised. This is the situation at the bottom of the geyser's pit. Here the weight of the water above pushes down on the lower water, increasing its boiling point to well above 212° F. The temperature of this water, then, can increase tremendously before boiling occurs.

Eventually, as the temperature of the water increases, the temperature of some part of the complicated underground water system will go above even the higher boiling point, and some of the water will turn to steam. A large bubble of steam finds its way upwards to the surface of the pool and escapes. As it explodes from the water, some of the liquid will be carried with it and splash over the edge of the pool.

Now the pool contains less water, and the pressure on the water below is reduced a little. This lowers the boiling point of the water in the pit, and a tremendous amount of steam is suddenly produced. As the mass of steam rushes up the tube, it carries the cooler water with it. The result is a violent explosion of water and steam from the surface pool.

Some geysers are famous for the amount of water they throw into the air. One geyser in New Zealand throws water to a height of almost 1000 feet, throwing out enough water to supply a fairly large city. Other geysers are noted for the fact that they erupt on a regular schedule. In Yellowstone Park, Old Faithful has erupted once each hour, on the average, for many years, while the Great Geyser of Iceland erupted every thirty minutes for over a hundred years.

The pattern of geyser eruptions does change somewhat over a long period of time. Old Faithful is not quite as "faithful" as it used to be, taking long spells in which it does not perform on schedule. The Great Geyser became completely inactive about 50 years ago, because the level of the water at the top of the pool had fallen below the rim of rock around it. Thus, when a bubble of steam escaped, water could not splash out of the pool and relieve the pressure. As an experiment, a tube was cut through the rock so some of the water could be removed from the top of the pool. Immediately the geyser again began throwing water 200 feet into the air. But it has never returned to a regular schedule.

When we consider all of the conditions that determine just when and how much a geyser will erupt, it is not surprising that its patterns change. The timing of a geyser must depend upon the amount of heat flowing into the water at the bottom of the pit and the speed with which water enters the pit. If either of these changes even a little, the time that it takes for the temperature and pressure of the geyser to reach just the right point for eruption will certainly change.

HOT SPRINGS

In addition to its 200 geysers, Yellowstone Park also contains over 3000 hot springs. Others are scattered throughout the U.S., with one concentration of 47 in Hot Springs National Park in central Arkansas. Hundreds of hot springs are found in Iceland. There the hot water is used to heat homes and buildings. Like geysers, hot springs may be found near any area of recent volcanic activity.

Surrounded by the steam from
hot springs in the Yellowstone National Park, Wyoming,
are interesting rock formations.

The structure of a hot spring is similar to that of a geyser, except that the water passage must be much more simple. Since a hot spring never explodes, scientists assume that the passageway is not crooked and branched like that of a geyser, but instead is fairly straight. The water near the bottom of the spring must be close to a mass of magma, from which it gets its heat. The hot water must then be free to rise upward before it turns to steam, and the cooler water at the top must be free to circulate to the bottom where it is heated.

Hot springs may have temperatures at or near the boiling point of water, 212° F. Those in Hot Springs, Arkansas, are all about 145° F, and a half a million people visit the park each year in order to bathe in the warm water.

PAINT POTS

Paint pots are simply hot springs that contain mud that makes their water cloudy and often very thick. Their name comes from the fact that the mud is often highly colored by various minerals.

The hot water of areas like Yellowstone Park will dissolve many minerals that are found in the ground. These minerals are carried to the surface by the water and, as the water evaporates in the air the minerals are left as solid materials on the rocks. Or, as in the case of the paint pots, the minerals remain in the water, coloring it with brilliant hues. Most paint pots are blue-gray in color, although some are various shades of red and yellow. Around most geysers, hot springs, and paint pots are rims of solid, smooth minerals left by the evaporating water. Surprisingly enough, microscopic plants and animals manage to live in some of the hot springs, adding their variety of color to that of the sulfur and iron.

DRY SPRINGS

Occasionally a spring or a geyser will become dry during a drought. When this happens, gases may flow through the dry pool. These gas jets are called *fumaroles*.

Usually the gases from fumaroles are made up mostly of steam. However, the smell of sulfur in the air around them tells us that other gases are sometimes mixed with the steam.

Fumaroles, holes in the earth from which gases escape, line the Firehole River in the Yellowstone National Park.

CHAPTER THIRTEEN

WINDOWS INTO THE EARTH

WHAT DO YOU THINK of when the word "volcano" is mentioned? Most people think of a huge mountain, perhaps with a column of smoke coming from its top. But not all volcanoes form mountains. Some volcanic eruptions come from fairly flat ground. The important part of a volcano is the opening or vent from the surface of the earth to a melted mass or rock which is generally no deeper than 40 miles. This vent is the "window" through which scientists have learned so much about the center of our planet.

Scientists have learned a great deal more about the sun and the moon than they have about the center of the earth. The deepest oil wells reach only about five miles into the earth. These are but pin-pricks in the surface of our planet, which is almost 8000 miles in diameter. You can easily understand why scientists are excited when a volcano begins to throw out materials from 40 miles below.

The drilling of oil wells and the digging of mines have revealed that the temperature of the earth increases the deeper we go. No one really knows why this happens. The amount of this increase in temperature varies at different places on the earth, but it averages about one Fahrenheit degree for every 60 feet of depth. In other words, at one mile below the surface, we would expect the temperature to be about 150° F, and at ten miles the temperature might be well over 1000° F! And, at depths below 20 miles, it is probably well above the melting point of most rocks.

Scientists have been able to perform several types of experiments which seem to show that rocks at the center of the earth are *not* liquid, in spite of the high temperature that must exist there. They think this is true because of the very high pressure at the center of the earth, caused by the weight of the rocks above. When a crack appears in the surface crust of the earth, this pressure is reduced and the rocks far below the surface at that point may become soft enough to flow.

In some way that scientists do not yet understand, the heat from the center of the earth melts some of the rock nearer the surface of the earth—say some 30 or 40 miles down. This mass is apparently made not only of melted rock, but also of many kinds of gases that are dissolved in the melted rock. The whole thing—the liquid rock and the gases in it—is called magma as long as it is under the ground.

Since the magma is fairly near the surface of the earth, it begins to cool a little. As it does, the gases in it, which are mostly steam, separate from the rock and begin to build up tremendous pressures. Because of these pressures, the magma begins to move—sometimes sideways but more often upward, following weak places in the rocks. As it nears the surface of the earth, the weight of the rocks above and the temperature of the magma both become less. As a result, more and more gas escapes, and the pressure inside the magma becomes very great. You have seen the force of gas escaping from a liquid when you open a bottle of soda pop. Before you remove the cap, the gases are dissolved in the liquid, but once the pressure is removed, out they come!

Usually, by the time the magma reaches the surface, it has lost most of the gases that were dissolved in it. From this point on, the scientists refer to it as lava. Lavas are of two general types. Some, such as those produced by Parícutin, are quite thick, like toothpaste. These pasty lavas are usually light in color. Since they do not flow easily, they form very rough, broken, jagged flows. The other type of lava will often produce flat fields with smooth or only slightly wrinkled surfaces, since it is very thin and flows readily.

TYPES OF VOLCANOES

As you have seen from reading this book, no two volcanoes act exactly alike. But scientists can recognize several different types. You have already read about most of these.

The *Pelean* type of volcano, named after Mount
Pelée, can be the most dangerous, since it often explodes
without warning. In this type of volcano the magma is so
thick it cannot flow at all. As the steam and other gases
escape and the pressure builds higher and higher, the
almost-solid magma is pushed upward through the
vent. Because of this, the vent becomes almost completely clogged and the gases cannot escape.

Finally the pressure becomes so great that a violent
explosion takes place, usually tearing a hold in the side
of the cone. The glowing cloud that is usually formed
by the Pelean type of volcano is made up of the hot gases
that were at one time dissolved in the magma. As in the
case of Mount Pelée, the cloud is often heavier than
air and follows the slope of the cone downward, killing
everything on the ground. Occasionally, the glowing
cloud will be light enough to rise upward into the air,
and very little damage will be done.

The *Vesuvian* type of eruption was named for Mount
Vesuvius. Krakatoa is another example of this type of
volcano, even though it is under water.

The first sign that a Vesuvian volcano has "come
alive" again is the release of a tremendous amount of
gas. This shows that the magma is moving, cooling
down, and releasing gases. Often a small cone will be
built up around the mouth of the vent, made of the
ash and cinders that have been brought up by the
escaping steam.

This is followed by a flow of rather thick lava, which
cools almost immediately and clogs the mouth of the
vent. For several days, or perhaps several months, the
volcano will lie quietly. But beneath the surface more

gases are escaping from the magma. They cannot escape through the vent and into the open air because of the now-solid lava that blocks the opening. Finally, a tremendous explosion occurs, throwing huge amounts of ash, cinders, blocks, and bombs into the air. Once the pressure is released, the Vesuvian volcano goes into a long resting stage, and slowly begins to build up strength for its next explosion.

A third type of volcano is named for the 3000-foot-high mountain, Stromboli. This volcano forms a tiny island in the Mediterranean Sea off the coast of Sicily, and has been in almost constant eruption for the last 2500 years! Because of this, Stromboli has been called "The Lighthouse of the Mediterranean."

Violent explosions from *Strombolian* type volcanoes are rare. This is because the magma is very, very fluid and hot enough so it never becomes completely solid. The escaping steam causes many small, frequent explosions that rarely do more than throw the glowing lava into the air. The steam cloud hangs over the top of the mountain almost constantly and reflects the glow from the lava that fills the crater below it. At night, this glow can be seen for miles in all directions, warning ships of the presence of the island. This is how Stromboli got its nickname.

Mauna Lao and Kilauea, in Hawaii, produce lava that is even less thick than that of the Strombolian type volcanoes. *Hawaiian* type volcanoes rarely explode violently. Instead, they produce large flows of thin, rope-like lava that spread out to form a large shield.

The last type of volcano is named the *Icelandic* type,

although much of the volcanic activity of the north-western United States was also of this type. We have very few good descriptions of this type of flow, since the last one occurred in Iceland in 1783. Even so, scientists have still succeeded in discovering many things about Icelandic volcanoes.

The lava from this type of volcano is very thin, much like that from the Hawaiian type. The major differences between these two types are the type of vents from which the lava flows, and the amounts of lava produced. In the Icelandic type of volcano, many huge fissures are produced, rather than a single (or at most, a few) small vent. From these large cracks in the ground, tremendous amounts of lava pour out. This thin lava flows out evenly over the land around the fissures, filling the valleys and covering the hills. When it cools, the lava forms a large area of flat land called a plateau that may be tens of thousands of square miles in size.

TYPES OF CONES

As you might expect, volcanoes produce different types of mountains, depending upon what happens to the cone as it is being formed. If, like Parícutin, the volcano produces mostly tephra, a cinder cone may be produced. Since these mountains are made almost entirely of material that fell to the ground in solid form, their sides are often quite steep—sometimes as steep as 40 degrees with the horizon. How steep they are depends mostly upon the size of the particles that formed the cone. You can experiment with this by letting sand fall slowly through your fingers from about a foot or so

Cinder cones such as this one found in the Canadian Kastline Plateau are formed when tephra is thrown from a volcano as it erupts.

off the ground. You will discover that the shape of each "cone" you build will be almost the same, regardless of its size. "Cinder cones" are formed in much the same way but using larger particles (such as gravel) or smaller particles (such as flour) will give you mountains with different shapes.

The islands of Hawaii are formed in another way. Here the volcano vents produced very little tephra. Instead, the islands were formed almost entirely from lava flows. Since the lava was fairly fluid, the mountains have gently sloping sides, and are almost always much wider at the base than they are high. These are called *shield volcanoes*.

Most of the volcanic mountains in the world seem to be a mixture of both cinder cones and shield volcanoes. Scientists call these types *composite cones*. Sometimes they are called *strato-volcanoes*, since they are made of alternating layers of cinders and lava flows.

Most of the world's largest volcanoes are of the composite type. You have probably heard of Mount Fujiyama in Japan or Africa's Kilimanjaro. The slopes of the sides of mountains of this type are not as steep as those of cinder cones, or as gentle as those of shield volcanoes.

WHAT GOOD ARE VOLCANOES?

You have read about the destructive power of volcanoes. They have buried dozens of villages and cities beneath tons of lava or ash. They have killed a large number of people and a much larger number of animals and plants. But think for a minute about the *good* that can result because of volcanoes.

Farmers who live on the sides of volcanoes do so because their crops grow well there. The ash that is spread over the countryside by an active volcano is usually quite rich in certain minerals that plants need in order to grow. So, as soon as the ground has cooled enough, many brave people will move back to raise crops in order to take advantage of the fertile soil produced by the mountain.

In Iceland and some other places in the world, the heat of underground magmas has been used for several purposes. It is used to heat homes and factories. It provides heated water for bathing. And, in a few places, volcanic energy is used to run machinery.

The vents and fissures of volcanoes extend deep into the crust of the earth. Once in a while some very valuable materials are brought close enough to the surface for men to reach them. In Japan, for example, solid sulfur is taken from extinct volcanoes. Lead, zinc, mercury, tin, gold, and many other useful metals are often found near volcanic regions.

It may be that all of the diamonds in the world were formed inside active volcanoes. A diamond is a pure form of carbon and is often found in the vents of volcanoes. Scientists have discovered that a diamond can be made in the laboratory if a bit of carbon is put under a great deal of pressure and heat. Both of these conditions would be created by an active volcano.

The rocks that are produced by a volcano can be useful in themselves. Perhaps you have used soap that contains ground-up lava. Certainly your dentist has used pumice to clean your teeth.

But to many of us, the most valuable thing about volcanoes is the beautiful and exciting scenery they produce. Smooth, pleasant-looking mountains and hills are often volcanic cones. Many of the islands of the world, including the beautiful ones of our newest state, Hawaii, were formed by volcanic action. The fantastic geysers, hot springs, and paint pots that are found in many parts of the world would not be available for us to look at if it were not for a buried mass of magma somewhere below. The Palisades that line parts of the Hudson River, Shiprock in New Mexico, the Craters of the Moon Park, and hundreds of other similar structures are reminders of our volcanic past.

RINGS OF FIRE

You have read stories about famous volcanoes that were located in the Mediterranean Sea, in the West Indies, and near Java. Others were found in Hawaii, Iceland, Mexico, the Philippines, and the western United States and Alaska. In addition, we have mentioned other volcanoes in Japan and Africa.

The volcanoes mentioned in this book are only a few of the hundreds of active and thousands of inactive volcanoes in the world. The major ones of these are shown on the map on the endpapers at the front and rear of the book.

It doesn't take too long to see a pattern in the location of volcanoes in the world. This pattern gives us a clue to the cause of volcanoes.

There are two fairly complete "rings of fire" around the earth. The first and most complete ring circles the Pacific Ocean. Volcanoes are quite common along the Pacific coast of South America, Central America, and North America. They form an almost-continuous chain down the other side of the Pacific, from Alaska and Siberia through Australia. This "ring of fire" includes Parícutin, Mount Lassen, The Valley of Ten Thousand Smokes, Fujiyama, Krakatoa, and Taal, as well as many other volcanoes that have not been discussed in this book.

The second volcanic "ring of fire" runs roughly parallel to the equator. Although it is not as complete as the "ring" around the Pacific, this belt of volcanoes seems to run through the Mediterranean Sea, through Indonesia, back up to Hawaii and down through Mexico and the West Indies. Notice that many famous volcanoes lie within this "ring." These include Mount Vesuvius, Stromboli, and Thera in the Mediterranean area, as well as the Hawaiian Islands and Mount Pelée. Near the place where this "ring" crosses the one that surrounds the Pacific Ocean, we find the most terrible of all volcanoes—Taal and Krakatoa among them.

Scientists have found regions of the world where mountains have been pushed up most recently. The Mid-Atlantic Ridge, a huge mountain chain that lies at the bottom of the Atlantic Ocean, is one of these new mountain uplifts. The islands of Iceland are the tops of some of these peaks, which have been pushed up until they extend through the surface of the water. Surtsey and the many volcanoes of Iceland are the result of the rise of these mountains.

These mountains, like almost all of the earth's mountains, were formed by forces deep within the earth that caused the surface to wrinkle into huge folds. The mountains, the volcanoes that occur near them, and the belts of eathquake activity also found here, are probably caused by the same forces. Through the study of volcanoes, scientists hope to understand these forces better.

Mt. Shishaldin is an active Alaskan volcano.
Even its glacial exterior cannot hide
the warning of the smoking peak.

ACKNOWLEDGEMENTS

Photographs in this book are reproduced courtesy of the following institutions:

page 25: The Bettmann Archive, Inc.

pages 35, 47, 54–55, 69, 72–73, 106–107: United Press International Photo

pages 96–97, 137: Field Museum of Natural History

pages 118–119: Black Star

pages 126–127: Wide World Photos

pages 129, 130: H. Armstrong Roberts

pages 132–133, 160–161: Authenticated News International

page 139: David W. Corson from A. Devaney, N.Y.

pages 144, 146–147: A. Devaney, Inc., N.Y.

page 155: British Columbia Government Photograph

GLOSSARY

Altitude Height above sea level.

Amphitheater An oval or circular outdoor auditorium, used by the ancient Romans as a theater.

Apollo A young, handsome god of both the ancient Greeks and Romans.

Aqueduct A man-made canal or passageway for water.

Archeology The scientific study of ancient people.

Ash, volcanic Solid material less than 1/6 of an inch long that is blown from a volcano.

Barometer A scientific instrument used to measure and, sometimes, to record the pressure of the air.

Bearing   The calculation of the position of something by finding its direction and distance from a fixed point.

Block, volcanic   A large solid rock thrown from a volcano. (compare with *bomb*)

Bomb, volcanic   A large rock that is thrown from a volcano in liquid form. Many bombs become solid before they reach the ground. (compare with *block*)

Caldera   A pit, more than one mile across, found at the top of some volcanic mountains; usually formed by the explosive blowing-out of volcanic material followed by the collapse of the mountain top into the space the material formerly occupied.

Capsize   To turn over or upset.

Carbon dioxide   A heavy, colorless gas formed by the chemical combination of carbon with oxygen.

Caribou   A large deer, found in northern North America, related to the reindeer.

Carlsbad Cavern   A large cave in southern New Mexico.

Char   To change to charcoal by burning or scorching.

Charcoal   A form of carbon made by heating wood to a high temperature in the absence of oxygen.

Cinder   A solid particle between 1/6 and 1 1/2 inches long that is thrown from a volcano.

Condense   To change a gas to a liquid.

Cone, volcanic   A general term for a volcanic mountain or hill.

Corrugated   Any material the surface of which has been formed into a series of ridges.

Crater   A pit less than one mile across found at the top of some volcanic mountains, formed by the explosive blowing-out of material.

Crater lake (general)   A lake of water formed in the bottom of a crater.

Crust (of the earth)   The outer solid "skin" of the earth, usually less than 40 miles thick.

Crystallization   The process of forming crystals of a substance by the evaporating of the solvent in which it is dissolved.

Cubic mile   A measure of volume, being a cube one mile wide, one mile long, and one mile deep.

Debris   A collection of loose rock fragments; rubbish.

Dinghy   A small rowboat.

Disintegrate   To break into smaller particles.

Dissolve   To mix two or more substances so as to make a solution. For example, when salt is mixed with water, the salt is *dissolved* and a salt water solution is formed.

Dust, volcanic   Very small, often microscopic particles of solid material blown from a volcano.

Earthquake   A shaking or trembling of the earth.

Eruption   The sudden, often violent, release of liquids, gases, or solids by a volcano or geyser.

Evacuate   To remove a group of people from a dangerous area.

Evaporate   To change a liquid into a gas.

Excavate   To uncover by digging.

Extinct   In the case of a volcano, no longer active and not expected to ever become active again. If speaking of plants or animals, no longer living.

Filter   To remove unwanted materials; to strain.

Fissure   Any natural opening in the earth that is longer than it is wide; a crack in the surface of the earth. (compare with *vent*).

Fluid   Any material that will flow; not solid; may be a gas but is usually a liquid.

Fluorine   An element that is pale yellow and poisonous for us to breathe in its gaseous form. Sometimes released during volcanic eruptions.

Forum   The market place or open square where ancient Romans held public meetings.

Fumarole   An opening in the earth through which only gases escape.

Geologist   A scientist who studies the earth.

Geyser   A hot spring that occasionally erupts, throwing water and steam into the air.

Gladiator   A man who fought against other gladiators or against wild animals as entertainment for the ancient Romans.

"Glowing cloud"   A cloud made of a mixture of gases and glowing solid particles produced by a volcano. Usually heavier than air.

Hot spring   A pool of water that is heated from an underground mass of molten rock.

Inactive   A volcano that has not erupted recently and shows few signs of erupting again. The use of this word indicates that scientists are not certain that the volcano is extinct yet.

Infrared   Invisible waves of energy given off by hot objects.

Jet Stream   A current of wind found in the stratosphere, often blowing at speeds of up to 250 mph, usually from the west.

Lava   Molten rock that has lost most of its gases, and has been pushed out onto the surface of the earth.

Magma   An underground molten mass, composed of melted rock with various gases (mostly steam) dissolved in it.

Mammoth Cave   The largest single cave in the world, located in central Kentucky.

Microscopic   Too small to be seen without the use of a microscope.

Molten   Melted; made liquid by heat.

Mosaic   Decoration made, in Pompeii, by setting colored pebbles into a surface to form a design or picture.

"Muddy cloud"   A cloud of the type sometimes produced by the Taal Volcano, composed of gases and particles of mud. It is highly acid and "burns" upon contact with the skin.

Mudflow   A mass of mud that is thin enough to flow downhill.

Mud pot   A hot spring in which enough mud has been dissolved to make the water cloudy.

Mural   A picture painted directly on a wall or other surface.

Nautical mile   Approximately 6076 feet.

Observatory, volcano   A place from which scientists study volcanoes.

Oxygen   The most abundant of the chemical elements on earth. Burning is the rapid combining of oxygen with another material. Almost all living things require a constant supply of oxygen.

Particle   A very small part of anything; any of the pieces of a broken rock.

Pendulum   An object suspended from a fixed frame-work so that it is free to swing.

Porous   Full of holes, like a sponge.

Pulverize   To crush or grind into small particles.

Pumice   A volcanic rock through which gas bubbled while the rock was still molten. Being full of holes, the rock is often light enough to float in water.

Ravine   A narrow, steep-sided valley, usually worn by running water.

Reflect   To bounce light (or heat or sound) from one surface to another.

Rejuvenate   To make young again.

Satellite, Weather   A man-made "moon" orbiting the earth to collect information about the weather. Some weather satellites take photographs of the earth while others carry infrared detectors. These can locate "hot spots" on the earth's surface.

Seismograph   A machine used by scientists to detect and record earthquakes.

Soil   A mixture of crushed rock, certain chemicals, and water which is capable of supporting the growth of plants.

Sterile   Containing nothing that is alive.

Stratosphere   The layer of the atmosphere which is about seven miles from the earth's surface.

Suffocation   To gasp for breath; to die from lack of oxygen.

Sulfur   A chemical element that is a yellow solid at normal temperatures. As a gas, sulfur has a very strong smell.

Sulfuric acid   A strong acid that contains sulfur, hydrogen and oxygen.

Summit   The highest point on a mountain.

Superheated   Very hot and dry gas; or a liquid that has been heated above its boiling point without boiling taking place.

Tephra   A single term for all of the solid materials, regardless of size, thrown from a volcano during an eruption.

Thermal   Having to do with heat; hot.

TNT   A high explosive.

Torrent   A violent stream of liquid, such as water or lava.

Tremor   A quivering or shaking.

Tsunamis   A sea wave caused by an earthquake.

Vent   A single, usually more-or-less round, opening in the earth.

Volcanologist   A geologist who specializes in the study of volcanoes.

INDEX

Billye and Walt Brown obviously have found a dispensation from the narrow confines of a 24-hour day. They need 26 hours, at least, to accommodate all their activities and interests. Besides writing books together, the Browns pursue independent careers: Billye is a free lance writer and editor; Walt is a teacher. In her spare time, Billye helps a Girl Scout troop in producing a newspaper, serves on a public relations committee for the Girl Scouts, and teaches a course in "Decision Making" for young people in her church. Not to be outdone, Walt spends his free time as president of the neighborhood PTA and as superintendent of his church's Sunday School.

On a recent trip to Europe, Billye Brown almost made it to the island of Surtsey—but the weather didn't cooperate. She consoled herself by collecting lava specimens in Iceland. Then, she made for Mt. Vesuvius in Italy. There was nothing to stop her from clambering up over the mountain's summit and down into the crater. Then a side trip to Pompeii made a perfect conclusion to her expedition.

KRAKATOA   VESU

STROMBOLI

MT. LASSEN

KATMAI   HAWAII

Two "rings of fire" locate some of the major volcanoes in the world. One ring circles the Pacific Ocean while the second ring runs almost parallel to the equator.